Overweight America

by Meryl Loonin

LUCENT BOOKS

An imprint of Thomson Gale, a part of The Thomson Corporation

Detroit • New York • San Francisco • San Diego • New Haven, Conn. • Waterville, Maine • London • Munich

To Neil, Hana, and Jonah.

LIBRARY OF CONGRESS CATALOGING-IN-PUBLICATION DATA

Loonin, Meryl.
  Overweight America / by Meryl Loonin.
    p. cm.— (Hot topics)
  Includes bibliographical references and index.
  Contents: Weight and health in America—Why are Americans overweight?—Eating habits and lifestyle among American youth—The role of the food industry—Changing attitudes and waistlines.
  ISBN 1-59018-744-X (hard cover : alk. paper) 1. Obesity—United States.
  I. Title. II. Series: Hot topics (San Diego, Calif.)
  RC628.L57 2006
  362.196'398--dc22

                                                                    2006004284

Printed in the United States of America

CONTENTS

FOREWORD

Young people today are bombarded with information. Aside from traditional sources such as newspapers, television, and the radio, they are inundated with a nearly continuous stream of data from electronic media. They send and receive e-mails and instant messages, read and write online "blogs," participate in chat rooms and forums, and surf the Web for hours. This trend is likely to continue. As Patricia Senn Breivik, the dean of university libraries at Wayne State University in Detroit, states, "Information overload will only increase in the future. By 2020, for example, the available body of information is expected to double every 73 days! How will these students find the information they need in this coming tidal wave of information?"

Ironically, this overabundance of information can actually impede efforts to understand complex issues. Whether the topic is abortion, the death penalty, gay rights, or obesity, the deluge of fact and opinion that floods the print and electronic media is overwhelming. The news media report the results of polls and studies that contradict one another. Cable news shows, talk radio programs, and newspaper editorials promote narrow viewpoints and omit facts that challenge their own political biases. The World Wide Web is an electronic minefield where legitimate scholars compete with the postings of ordinary citizens who may or may not be well-informed or capable of reasoned argument. At times, strongly worded testimonials and opinion pieces both in print and electronic media are presented as factual accounts.

Conflicting quotes and statistics can confuse even the most diligent researchers. A good example of this is the question of whether or not the death penalty deters crime. For instance, one study found that murders decreased by nearly one-third when the death penalty was reinstated in New York in 1995. Death penalty supporters cite this finding to support their argument that the existence of the death penalty deters criminals from committing murder. However, another study found that states without the death penalty have murder rates below the national average. This study is cited by opponents of capital punishment, who reject the claim that the death penalty deters murder. Students need context and clear, informed discussion if they are to think critically and make informed decisions.

The Hot Topics series is designed to help young people wade through the glut of fact, opinion, and rhetoric so that they can think critically about controversial issues. Only by reading and thinking critically will they be able to formulate a viewpoint that is not simply the parroted views of others. Each volume of the series focuses on one of today's most pressing social issues and provides a balanced overview of the topic. Carefully crafted narrative, fully documented primary and secondary source quotes, informative sidebars, and study questions all provide excellent starting points for research and discussion. Full-color photographs and charts enhance all volumes in the series. With its many useful features, the Hot Topics series is a valuable resource for young people struggling to understand the pressing issues of the modern era.

INTRODUCTION

When it comes to weight and health, the United States is a land of contradictions. This is clear at the checkout of any of the nation's major supermarkets. As shoppers wheel their carts to the front of the line, they are confronted on one side by glossy health and glamour magazines that show photos of super-thin celebrities and headlines that tout miracle diets ("Shed Four Pounds a Week!") and fitness workouts ("Be a Fat-Burning Success Story!"). On the other side are shelves lined with dozens of brands of candy, gum, and other high-calorie snack-food items, strategically placed for last-minute purchases. Americans are more obsessed with body image and diet than almost any other culture in the world, but they are also gaining weight faster than people in almost any other nation. As many as two-thirds of adults in the country—and one-sixth of children—are reported to be either overweight or obese (severely overweight), and the numbers grow larger each year. Health experts warn that the problem has become an epidemic.

Doctors and nutritionists have been sounding the alarm about the dangers of Americans' unhealthy diets and lack of exercise for decades, but the public has reacted with apathy and inaction. Many Americans believe that those who are obese are personally responsible for lacking the discipline and willpower to get in shape. The country's huge fast-food, snack-food, and soda industries have encouraged this belief. They have lobbied hard to persuade elected officials and the public that weight gain should remain a matter of private rather than public concern. As a result, the issue has remained low on the national agenda.

Only as weight gain and obesity have spread to Americans of all ages and income levels, and especially as more children and teens have been affected by it, has the problem become too widespread to ignore. In recent years, media coverage of the issue has exploded. It has become difficult to pick up a newspaper or turn on a TV news or talk show without hearing about an obesity crisis. Doctors, nutritionists, and politicians all speak out publicly on the issue of weight. Pharmaceutical companies devote tremendous resources and energy to the search for weight-loss drugs and treatments.

Yet many health experts believe that the key to the nation's obesity problem lies in the unhealthy—some even say toxic— environment in which Americans live, work, and spend their leisure time. It is an environment in which supersize portions are the norm and grocery stores stock a dizzying variety of snack foods, frozen desserts, and sugary cereals. Inducements to eat high-calorie foods are everywhere. U.S. children are exposed to junk-food commercials every time they tune in to their favorite TV programs. In many poor neighborhoods, it is much

Teens watch television while eating high calorie snacks.

easier to purchase a bag of Doritos chips or a box of Pop-Tarts toaster pastries than an apple or a tomato.

Life in America has also become increasingly sedentary. Cities sprawl across vast distances, forcing people to spend hours in their cars. Work is increasingly performed sitting in an office chair typing on a computer. Leisure time activities frequently involve sitting still, in front of a television or movie screen or logged onto a virtual world of computer and video games, Web sites, and chat rooms.

Is Obesity a Threat to the Nation?

Despite these trends, some social critics downplay the threat that obesity poses to the nation. They argue that Americans have

Young people often learn good eating habits—and bad eating habits—from their parents.

simply become victims of their own prosperity. Obesity and weight gain, they say, are problems that afflict nations of the world in which food is plentiful and affordable. "Not only has our remarkable economy managed to feed all of its citizens," writes libertarian policy analyst Radley Balko, an advocate for less government interference in people's lives, "our chief worry right now seems to be that our poor and middle class have *too much* to eat. That's a remarkable achievement."[1]

Nutritionists and health experts counter that obesity is linked to serious and life-threatening illnesses and disabilities that carry enormous economic and public health costs. Low-income Americans often bear a disproportionate share of the health burden. Although they suffer less frequently from the desperate hunger and malnutrition that plague people in the poorest nations of the world, they often lack access to nutritious foods, such as fruits and vegetables, that promote good health and protect against disease. "Listening to my young patients talk about their lives," says Francine Kaufman, a doctor who has treated many children with obesity-related diseases, "I become angry at a society that doesn't seem to care, at an economic structure that makes it cheaper to eat fries than fruit, and at the food industry and the mass media luring children to consume what should not be consumed."[2]

Health advocates such as Kaufman argue that Americans can no longer afford to be complacent about the nation's growing obesity problem or to treat extreme weight gain as solely a matter of personal responsibility. They insist that public and private institutions must play an active role in helping to reverse unhealthy diet and lifestyle trends that have taken hold over the past several decades. The goal, these advocates say, is to stop blaming the individuals in American society who become overweight or obese and instead work to bring about broader, more lasting changes in an environment that promotes weight gain and makes unhealthy eating and inactivity accepted ways of life.

WEIGHT AND HEALTH IN AMERICA

From nightly newscasts, to newsmagazines, to talk radio shows, the message is everywhere that Americans are gaining weight at an alarming pace. With a growing sense of urgency, doctors, scientists, and politicians have begun to warn that being over-weight or obese can lead to serious health risks such as heart disease and diabetes, and that obesity is costing the nation billions of dollars in medical care and hospital visits. U.S. Surgeon General Richard Carmona, one of the nation's most prominent public health officials, issued an impassioned call to action in 2004, telling the public that obesity is "every bit as threatening to us as is the terrorist threat we face today. It is the threat from within."[3]

Although extreme weight gain is rapidly becoming a world-wide trend, replacing malnutrition as the number one food problem in many parts of the world, the United States leads the way. Obesity is more widespread in the United States than anywhere else in the industrialized world. In a land in which bigger is often equated with better, Americans' waistlines are expanding along with the size of their cars, hamburgers, and soft drinks.

With breaking stories about diet and weight in the news almost daily, doctors and scientists are working to understand the threat that obesity poses to the nation. They attempt to track weight gain in the population, learn who is most affected by rising rates of obesity, and evaluate the real impact obesity has on Americans' long-term health and well-being.

Measuring Weight Gain and Obesity

The measure that most medical professionals use to determine if a person is overweight or obese is a ratio of weight and height called the body mass index (BMI). BMI is derived by dividing a person's weight in kilograms by his or her height in meters squared. (This converts to weight in pounds divided by height in inches squared, then multiplied by 703.) BMI is a quick and easy way to calculate how much body fat individuals carry relative to their height and whether they fall in a healthy weight range or one that puts them at high risk for developing weight-related illness. It can be obtained without elaborate equipment or training.

Many American teenagers are overweight because they eat poorly and do not get enough exercise.

All that's needed are an accurate scale and height-measuring rod. This makes it a practical means for scientists around the world to track and compare weight gain among different populations.

The U.S. government's Centers for Disease Control and Prevention (CDC) has established a normal range for BMI for adults of any height or shape. A BMI is considered normal if it falls between 18 and 25. This means that for a woman of average height, 5 feet 4 inches tall (163cm), a normal BMI translates to a weight of between 108 and 144 pounds (49 and 65kg). For a man of average height, 5 feet 9 inches tall (175cm), the normal range falls between 125 and 168 pounds (57 and 76kg). If an adult's BMI is between 25 and 29.9, the CDC guidelines place him or her in the overweight category. Any number 30 or higher is considered obese.

In recent years, health officials have promoted BMI as a way for people to assess their own weight status and set achievable weight-loss goals. Dozens of Web sites have sprung up that allow users to plug in their height and weight and calculate their own BMIs. Yet some people object to the reliance on BMI to measure and compare weight gain. They argue that using such limited information to determine a person's physical condition and health risks means that people who are relatively healthy may be mislabeled as overweight or obese. The problem, they say, is that BMI makes no distinction between body fat and lean body mass, or muscle. It does not take into account whether a person exercises regularly and where his or her fat is located on the body. Yet all of these can have a major impact on overall health.

Critics of BMI, including groups representing food and restaurant companies, often point out that fit and muscular celebrities and athletes such as basketball star Michael Jordan, California governor and bodybuilder Arnold Schwarzenegger, movie star Brad Pitt, and even President George W. Bush are all considered either overweight or obese based solely on their BMIs. (Many female celebrities, on the other hand, tend to fall below the normal range, in the underweight category.) Medical experts concede that BMI may be flawed, but they say it is still the most reliable tool they have to monitor patients' weight and risk of disease.

Standard measures of obesity are imperfect. Former basketball star Michael Jordan (the picture of good health in this 2006 photograph) would be considered overweight according to some measures.

BMI is also used to assess children's weight. However, it is interpreted differently, because children grow and develop in very different ways as they mature. A child's BMI is calculated with the formula used for adults, but there are no set ranges to indicate that he or she is underweight or overweight. Instead, children's BMIs are compared on growth charts with those of other children of the same age and gender. For example, if a ten-year-old girl has a BMI that falls in the 60th percentile of the growth chart, then her BMI is higher than 60 percent of girls her own age. Only when a child's BMI is at or above the 85th percentile of the growth chart for his or her height, gender, and age, is that child considered at risk for becoming overweight. Those who fall above the 95th percentile are considered overweight. The term *obese* is usually reserved for adults, since labeling a child as obese can lead to emotional problems and low self-esteem.

Trends in Americans' Weight and Diet

Using BMI as a measure, there is no question that a greater percentage of Americans are overweight than they were fifty, twenty, or even ten years ago. Results of a national health survey covering the years 1999–2002 show that an astonishing 65 percent, or more than 125 million American adults, are either overweight or obese. As many as 30 percent of American adults, or 60 million people, are obese. Most alarming to health officials is the fact that 9 million of these obese adults are severely obese, which means they weigh 90 pounds (41kg) or more above the normal range for their height and gender. Weight gain and obesity among Americans are growing so fast that health surveys can hardly keep pace. Since the late 1970s, the percentage of obese adults has doubled—from 15 to 30 percent. "No other nation in history," says Eric Schlosser, author of the book *Fast Food Nation*, "has gotten so fat so fast."[4]

Obesity affects people in all segments of the U.S. population, in every state across the nation and among both sexes, regardless of age, race, or ethnic background. Increasingly, it affects people of all income and educational levels. Recent studies suggest that as of 2005, obesity is growing fastest among middle- and upper-income Americans who earn more than $60,000 a year.

Weight Gain Among Poor and Minority Americans

Despite the evidence that obesity is growing among wealthy Americans, health experts have known for decades that those who are most vulnerable to extreme weight gain and obesity are often poor. Economic and lifestyle factors play a role in ensuring that obesity and poverty go hand in hand. Healthy foods are typically more expensive than unhealthy foods and, therefore, more difficult for low-income people to afford. It is cheaper, for example, to buy a bag of Doritos chips than a pound of apples. There are also fewer places to purchase healthy foods in most poor neighborhoods. Many supermarket chains are reluctant to open stores in communities with high crime rates or visible signs of poverty such as homelessness. Instead, these neighborhoods often have an abundance of fast-food chains and small markets that sell high-calorie packaged foods. Residents of these neighborhoods not only have few healthy food options, they also often lack access to parks, playgrounds, bike paths, and other areas where they can safely walk and exercise.

Health experts say the large concentration of racial minorities and immigrant groups in many such poor communities

A sedentary lifestyle contributes to weight gain and puts the body at risk for serious health problems.

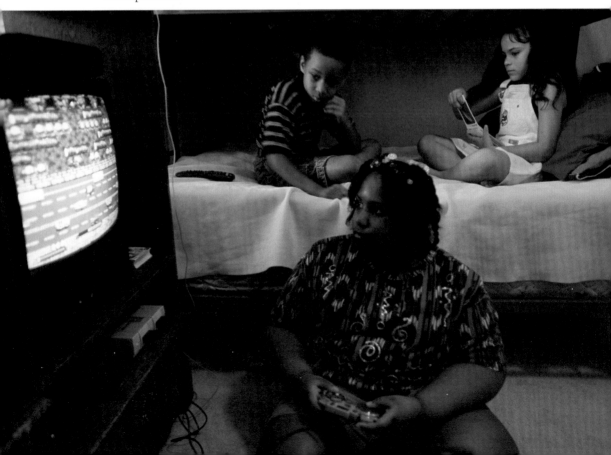

helps explain why African Americans, Latinos, and Native Americans have extremely high rates of excess weight and obesity. In 2000, nearly 70 percent of African American adults and 73 percent of Mexican American adults were estimated to be overweight or obese, compared to 62 percent of whites. Severe obesity is far more common among these minority racial groups than in the general population. In every region of the country, those who are the most likely to be severely obese and to suffer the accompanying reduced quality of life and physical illness are poor women from minority racial groups.

Weight Gain Among American Youth

Unhealthy diets and lifestyles are at the root of the obesity problem not only for poor and minority Americans but also for U.S. children of all income levels. The current generation of children in the United States is less fit and more prone to obesity than

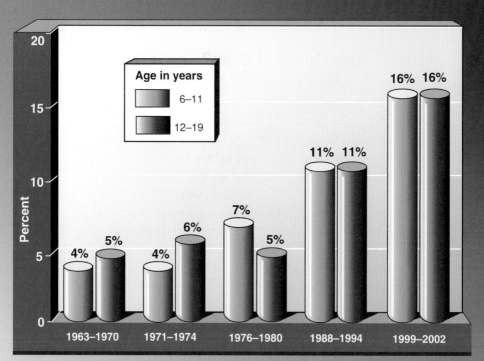

Percentage of Overweight Children and Adolescents (Ages 6–19)

The percentage of overweight children and adolescents was fairly stable from 1963 to 1980. From years 1976–1980 to years 1999–2002, it more than doubled for both groups.

any other generation in history. Roughly one in six U.S. children, or 16 percent, between the ages of six and nineteen is overweight. Another 15 percent are considered at risk for becoming overweight. The problem has become so widespread that the U.S. military has had to consider easing its weight standards for new teenage and young adult recruits. Many Americans of recruiting age simply weigh too much to be eligible. It is becoming a national security issue, as an Army nutrition specialist warns: "Unless weight rules are relaxed, we're going to have a harder time fielding an army."[5]

Surveys show that the children and teenagers most affected by obesity mirror those of the adult population. Children of African American, Latino, and Native American descent and those from low-income families are the most susceptible to extreme weight gain. In some heavily minority school districts, it is not unusual for as many as half of the students in a classroom to be overweight. A survey in New York City in 2003, for example, concluded that weight gain and obesity had reached epidemic proportions among children who attended the city's public schools. The problem was most pronounced in school districts with predominantly Latino and African American students, many of whom also come from low-income families.

What Causes Weight Gain?

Children and adults in the United States are becoming overweight because they consume more calories than they burn off in physical activity. Calories are the units used to measure the energy the body gets from food. This energy keeps people alive and moving and children growing. But when calorie intake is too high, excess food calories are stored as fat and people gain weight.

As anyone who has tried to lose weight knows, the human body is much more efficient at gaining weight than losing it. Scientists say this is the product of thousands of years of human prehistory. Ancient humans were hunter-gatherers who spent their days in intense physical activity. In harsh conditions or when food was scarce, they were forced to go for days or weeks at a time with barely enough food to sustain them. Those who could store food as body fat most efficiently when food was plentiful had a genetic advantage, because that excess fat could be converted to energy during the leaner times to keep them alive.

The result is that the body is genetically programmed to protect against weight loss at all costs and store extra energy as fat. That is why most people do not have to worry if they skip a meal or two. The average man or woman of normal weight has enough body fat to survive for weeks or even months without food. Yet the same biology that helped keep ancient humans from starving to death is poorly suited to modern conditions. Today's lifestyles are much more sedentary, and all it takes to gather food is a quick trip in the car to the supermarket. The modern environment, say Kelly Brownell and Katherine Battle Horgen, obesity experts and

When food was scarce for ancient hunter-gatherers, their stored fat sustained them. As a result, our modern genes are programmed to store fat.

Making Sense of Diet Advice: Fat and Carbs

The human body needs dietary fat for energy, but most Americans eat far more fat than their bodies can use. Some types of fat are worse for people's health than others.

Saturated fat is present in meats such as beef, pork, and lamb, and it is also in butter, cream cheese, mayonnaise, and salad dressing. Too much saturated fat boosts the "bad" cholesterol in the body and increases the risk of heart disease.

Trans fat is also closely linked to heart disease and obesity. It is a solid fat found in dairy and meat products, but it is also used heavily in packaged and fried foods. Food producers make trans fat by altering vegetable oils through a process called hydro-

genation. They use it because products made with it have a longer shelf life than products made with other fats. (Trans fat is often listed on food labels as hydrogenated vegetable oil.) Nutritionists advise that people consume healthier fats instead, such as those found in olive oil, peanut oil, and avocado.

Carbohydrates come in two main forms: sugars and starches. When people load up on carbs by eating snack foods, soda, and doughnuts, they are likely to gain weight. But the carbs in fruits and whole grains provide energy for physical activity and deliver important nutrients to the body.

authors of *Food Fight*, "will pound you with inducements to eat, make exertion unnecessary, and do little to defend you against diseases that most threaten you."[6] The only thing that keeps most people from overeating, they say, is sheer willpower.

Health Risks Linked to Obesity

For those who overeat and gain weight to the point of obesity, the health risks are often serious. Study after study confirms that obesity is linked to a wide range of health problems, including cancer, arthritis, and, chief among them, heart disease. People who carry excess weight often have elevated blood pressure and cholesterol levels, both of which can lead to heart disease or stroke.

High blood pressure (also called hypertension) refers to rising pressure against the walls of blood vessels. It causes the heart to work harder and can eventually damage other organs, such as the brain and kidneys. Although some people are genetically prone to high blood pressure, the condition is aggravated by factors such as excess body fat and a sedentary lifestyle. People who eat a diet high in fat and low in dietary fiber (which comes from foods such as fruits and vegetables) are also at risk for developing high LDL or so-called bad cholesterol levels. LDL deposits form on the walls of arteries, making it harder for the heart to pump blood, and this, too, boosts the chances of heart disease.

Diabetes is another serious illness that is closely tied to obesity. In simple terms, it is a condition in which the body has difficulty turning food into energy. Diabetes takes two forms, type 1 and type 2. Type 1 most often occurs in children and is usually inherited. It is dangerous and difficult to treat, but it is also fairly rare. Type 2, on the other hand, usually develops later in life and is linked to factors such as excess weight gain, an unhealthy diet, and a sedentary lifestyle.

A MAJOR THREAT

"Obesity, diabetes, and other diseases caused by poor diet and sedentary lifestyle now affect the health, happiness, and vitality of millions of men, women, and, most tragically, children and pose a major threat to the health care resources of the United States."

Kelly D. Brownell and Katherine Battle Horgen, *Food Fight: The Inside Story of the Food Industry, America's Obesity Crisis, & What We Can Do About It.* Chicago: McGraw-Hill Contemporary Books, 2004, p. 3.

Both types of diabetes involve problems in the way the body processes glucose, a sugar that comes from carbohydrates, which are the sugars and starches in food. Glucose is the body's main source of fuel. It provides the energy for every thought or movement humans make. But to use glucose, the body must first have a hormone called insulin, which is produced in the pancreas. In type 1 diabetes, the body is unable to make insulin. In type 2, the body produces insulin, but it either makes too little of it or it becomes resistant to it. The glucose accumulates in the

Is Obesity in the Genes?

Some people in the modern food environment stay thin, while others feel like they gain weight just by looking at a hamburger and fries. Modern humans have all inherited the same basic biology, but some may be genetically more prone to obesity. Genes affect metabolism, the rate at which people convert food into energy. They determine whether bodies put on fat easily or resist fat loss. They also play a role in the nervous energy, restless pacing, and other unconscious activities that help some people burn calories more readily than others.

Genes may also help to explain the high rate of obesity and diabetes among some racial groups in America. The ancient ancestors of African American and some Native American groups lived in harsh conditions where starvation loomed as a constant threat. Scientists suggest that their descendents may have inherited a "thrifty genotype," a genetic makeup that helped people obtain extra energy from small amounts of food and store away fat. This genotype was critical to survival in ancient times, but it may make people more prone to obesity now that food is readily available in supermarkets, restaurants, drive-through windows, and vending machines.

Genetics may explain why Native Americans, including this young Cherokee woman, are prone to obesity and diabetes.

blood, causing blood sugar levels to rise dangerously high and damaging tissues and blood vessels. Diabetes is the sixth-leading cause of death in the United States. It can devastate nearly every system of the body and cause heart disease, stroke, kidney failure, blindness, and painful nerve damage.

In recent years the rate of type 2 diabetes in the United States has soared along with the rate of obesity. Close to 90 percent of people with diabetes have type 2, and the vast majority of these people are overweight or obese. An estimated 18 million American adults are believed to have diabetes. And health experts warn that more than two times as many people may have higher than normal blood sugar levels, a sign that they are at risk for developing the disease. Minority groups with high rates of obesity have been particularly hard hit. African American adults are almost 1.6 times more likely, and Mexican American and Native American adults more than 2 times as likely, to have diabetes than white Americans. Doctors fear that within a generation, a huge wave of new diabetes cases may overwhelm the public health-care system.

The Stigma of Being Overweight

Although diabetes and other health risks associated with obesity are serious, some experts argue that the emotional and psychological damage caused by obesity may be even more traumatic. American culture idolizes super-thin models and celebrities. Advertisers target consumers with images that make many people dissatisfied with their bodies. Diet and weight advice is everywhere in magazines, best-selling books, and TV talk shows. In a society that places so much emphasis on staying slender, people who are obese often experience shame, anxiety, or depression. Some extremely overweight people become caught in a vicious cycle in which they feel depressed or angry and then eat for emotional reasons to feel better, only to end up feeling worse. Others become so desperate to lose weight that they fall prey to dangerous weight-loss schemes and diet pills or develop hazardous eating disorders that take a terrible toll on their physical health.

Obesity can also have a devastating impact on social lives, marriages, and academic and professional opportunities. Many employers are reluctant to hire a severely overweight worker for

Effects of Diabetes

People who are obese face serious health risks, including diabetes. The sixth leading cause of death in the United States, the disease can devastate nearly every system in the body, although if it is detected early, type 2 diabetes can often be controlled with diet and exercise, or medication.

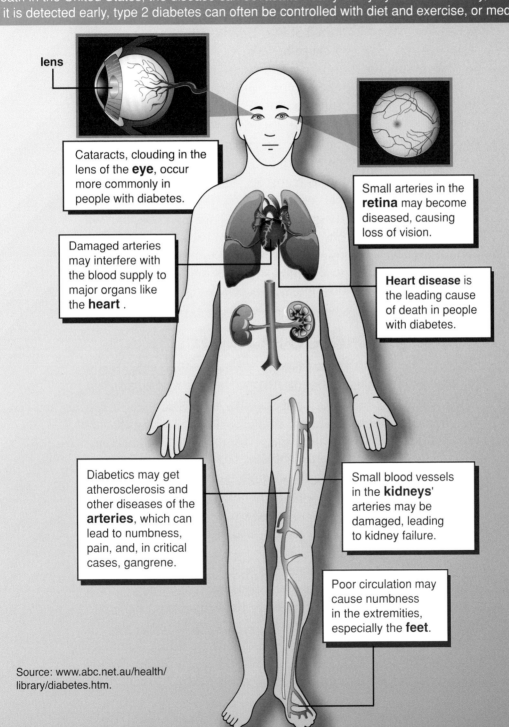

lens

Cataracts, clouding in the lens of the **eye**, occur more commonly in people with diabetes.

Small arteries in the **retina** may become diseased, causing loss of vision.

Damaged arteries may interfere with the blood supply to major organs like the **heart** .

Heart disease is the leading cause of death in people with diabetes.

Diabetics may get atherosclerosis and other diseases of the **arteries**, which can lead to numbness, pain, and, in critical cases, gangrene.

Small blood vessels in the **kidneys**' arteries may be damaged, leading to kidney failure.

Poor circulation may cause numbness in the extremities, especially the **feet**.

Source: www.abc.net.au/health/library/diabetes.htm.

fear of how it will reflect on the company's image. Obese job applicants often recount having encouraging conversations with potential employers over the phone, but then being quickly dismissed when they appear in person for a job interview. One study examined the effects of obesity on economic status and found that obese women, in particular, were more likely to have lower-paying jobs or to be unemployed than those with BMIs in the normal range. They were also more likely to marry men with lower incomes.

For overweight children, the psychological harm inflicted by relentless teasing, bullying, and social stigmatization can lead to a lifetime of body hatred, low self-esteem, anxiety, and even depression. Extremely overweight children may be repeatedly excluded from social groups, sports teams, or birthday parties. Some refuse to take part in physical education classes or other sports activities for fear of being teased or bullied. Others develop eating disorders or become yo-yo dieters, constantly losing weight and then gaining it back again.

Controversy Over Weight Studies

Despite the evidence that obesity is linked to serious health and emotional risks, some critics argue that the dire warnings about an obesity epidemic in the United States are exaggerated. They say the nation is obsessed with dieting and weight loss for cosmetic rather than legitimate health reasons. "Americans are enjoying longer lives and better health than ever before," writes *The Obesity Myth* author Paul Campos. "The claim that four out of five of us are running serious health risks because of our weight sounds exactly like the sort of exaggeration that can produce a cultural epidemic of fear, bearing no relation to any rational assessment of risk."[7]

At the center of this debate are studies in which scientists have attempted to link obesity to early death. Identifying such a link is difficult, however, because death certificates list the disease that is the immediate cause of death, such as diabetes or heart failure, and rarely mention obesity. This forces scientists to rely on surveys and make educated guesses about how many deaths are directly related to excess weight gain.

Although obesity is a major issue for many Americans, including this youngster, some critics say the problem has been exaggerated.

In March 2004, controversy erupted with the release of a widely publicized CDC report that claimed that as many as four hundred thousand deaths every year in the United States could be linked to obesity, making it the second-leading cause of death after cigarette smoking. Media coverage of the obesity crisis exploded. TV and newspaper reports warned that Americans were killing themselves with a knife and fork.

Yet just a year later, the CDC admitted that the methods used in the study were flawed and revised the number of annual obesity-related deaths dramatically downward first to 26,000 and then to 112,000. The revised report even suggested that modestly overweight people may live longer on average than those in the normal or underweight BMI ranges. Groups representing the food industry were quick to comment on the new results. A spokesman for the industry group Center for Consumer Freedom wrote, "While government officials insist America is suffering from an epidemic of obesity, it's more like an epidemic of obesity myths."[8]

THE AMERICAN EXPERIENCE

"The American experience merely parallels what is happening all over the world; economic development invariably leads to less malnutrition, a more sedentary lifestyle, higher rates of obesity—and far longer life expectancy."

Paul Campos, *The Obesity Myth: Why America's Obsession with Weight Is Hazardous to Your Health*. New York: Gotham, 2004, p. 122.

Health advocates such as Brownell and Battle Horgen caution that people should not focus on the controversy over obesity-related deaths and lose sight of the larger problem. They say that obesity did not become a critical issue simply because it has been hyped in the media. It is of major concern because millions of people are affected by it, its health and emotional effects are serious, treatments are costly and often do not work, and the behaviors linked to it—poor eating habits and a lack of physical activity—are themselves contributors to ill health.

WHY ARE AMERICANS OVERWEIGHT?

French cuisine is known for its rich, creamy desserts and sauces. A popular German dish consists of thick sausages dripping with mustard. In many Dutch cities, street vendors sell cones of french fries with a heavy mayonnaise dipping sauce. Although these national foods are high in calories and fat, few diet books in European countries make the best-seller list, few people have heard of low-fat cookies or frozen Lean Cuisine dinners, and most grocery stores do not even stock nonfat milk. Yet obesity rates in Europe and most other regions of the world continue to lag behind that of the United States. Foreign visitors to U.S. shores often report that they are astounded by the large number of obese Americans they encounter at airports, restaurants, shopping malls, beaches, and popular tourist destinations like Disney World.

American culture and fast food are having a profound impact on the way people buy and consume food throughout the world. There are few nations where residents are unfamiliar with McDonald's burgers or Coca-Cola soda. Yet a unique mix of social and cultural forces in the United States—from a hugely profitable food industry that spends billions of dollars marketing its products to increasing leisure time spent in front of TVs and computer screens—has dramatically altered Americans' diets and lifestyles and set the stage for an obesity epidemic that outpaces most of the world. Americans live in an environment, say the authors of a 2005 study on obesity, in which it is hard not to become overweight.

An Abundance of Food Choices

The abundance of food is a major factor in the nation's growing weight problem. There is a greater quantity and variety of food in the United States than in any other culture in the history of the world. An estimated fifty-thousand food items are available to American consumers, compared to close to five-hundred a century ago. A visit to almost any local supermarket in the United States makes this readily apparent. These markets carry twelve times as many different food products as they did in the early 1960s. Shelves are lined with row after row of packaged foods, including snack items, sliced and shredded cheeses, yogurts with toppings and mix-ins, dozens of sugary breakfast cereals, and creamy frozen desserts. There are fourteen different varieties of Oreo cookies and more than thirty types of Lay's potato chips. "Is it any wonder," asks Campos, "that recent immigrants to the United States, when they first enter a supermarket, are said to sometimes wonder if they have stumbled into some sort of food museum?"[9]

Food is plentiful in America almost twenty-four hours a day, not only in supermarkets but also at shopping malls, airports, stadiums, drugstores, museums, and even schools and hospitals. Across the country, food can be purchased within short driving distances of most neighborhoods and along highway exits

Obesity is a bigger problem in the United States than in Europe, despite the European appetite for fatty foods such as these rich and elegant French desserts.

Contributing to America's obesity problem is the sheer abundance of food and the myriad of food products available on supermarket shelves.

at convenience stores, gas stations, and fast-food restaurants. The U.S. Department of Agriculture (USDA) estimates that when all the food currently available to the American public is divided by the total number of people in the country, the nation is producing more food per resident than ever before. Americans are also eating more than ever before. Studies of Americans' diets as well as data on the total number of calories in the food supply show a marked increase in consumption in every major food group since the 1970s.

Americans Eat More Packaged and Processed Foods

One of the most striking changes in Americans' eating habits is that they snack far more than in previous decades. According to food industry data, Americans average twenty food contacts per person each day, including snacks and meals. (In contrast, the French average seven food contacts per person each day.) This is largely due to the introduction of thousands of packaged and processed (or manufactured) food products into the U.S. market.

These foods are designed for convenience. They are available in single-serving-size packages or microwavable containers. They can be gulped down, often without a fork and spoon, in the car, at an office desk, or between classes at school. They include drinkable yogurts, cereal bars, potato chips, fruit leather, and lunches ready to go straight to school without any kitchen preparation time. Snack foods are becoming the number one selling grocery category in the country. The Snack Food Association, an industry group representing hundreds of U.S. companies that manufacture and supply snack-food items, estimates that Americans buy more than $32 billion worth of snack foods each year.

THE GOOD AND THE BAD

"There are no good or bad foods, only good or bad diets or eating styles. No single food or type of food ensures good health, just as no single food or type of food is necessarily detrimental to health."

The American Dietetic Association, "Total Diet Approach to Communicating Food and Nutrition Information," position paper, 2002. www.eatright.org/cps/rde/xchg/ada/hs. xsl/advocacy_adar_0102_ENU_HTML.htm.

Because they are so convenient to consume, these processed snacks and other food items have replaced fresh fruits, vegetables, and whole grains in many Americans' diets. People increasingly eat processed cheese and cheese spreads instead of cheese, and french fries and potato chips instead of potatoes. Processed foods are not just convenient, they also seem to offer good value for the dollar in comparison to fresh produce, fish, or meat, which can be expensive and time-consuming to prepare. For some low-income Americans, who live in communities where there are few if any grocery stores, processed foods may be their only choice. There may be nowhere to obtain fresh fruits and vegetables without traveling long distances on public transportation.

Yet although processed foods may seem like a bargain, nutritionists warn that they are a major contributor to rising rates of obesity. Even when these foods are marketed as healthful, they are often extremely high in sugar, fat, and sodium (contained in salt). Processed sugars, for example, are high on the ingredients list of a wide range of packaged foods from granola bars to canned soup. In Skippy Super Chunk peanut butter, sugar is second only to roasted peanuts on the ingredients list. Heinz ketchup lists high fructose corn syrup (a sweetener that is made from cornstarch and believed to promote fat growth) as the third ingredient after tomatoes and vinegar.

When foods are processed for packaging much of their dietary fiber is removed. Fiber is the bulky portion of plants or the starchiness in grains and beans that the body is unable to fully digest. It slows down the digestive process and makes people feel fuller and more satisfied. In many large studies, a high intake of fiber has been linked to a lower risk of heart disease.

Chips and other snacks, though tempting and tasty, have a lot of calories.

Portion Sizes Fit for a Tyrannosaurus Rex

Despite growing concern about obesity, supersizing remains one of the hottest trends in the food industry. The typical hamburger today weighs 5 ounces (28g) more than a hamburger in the 1950s and contains triple the calories (not including any cheese, bacon, or sauce). Bagels, muffins, and candy bars have become king-size and have correspondingly king-size calorie counts. French croissants baked in America are twice the size of croissants in Paris. French fry servings contain roughly 125 calories more than those sold in London. "Portion sizes in the States are already fit for a velociraptor and will soon measure up to the expectations of even the largest T. Rex," writes *The Fat of the Land* author Michael Fumento.

Food industry spokespersons say they are simply giving customers what they want. Yet inflated portions encourage people to eat more even if they are not hungry. Moviegoers eat more popcorn when they are given a larger container. People who buy M&M's candies in a larger bag consume as much as 70 percent more of the candy. Americans are easily persuaded that larger containers and supersize meals offer better value. But this is misleading. They pay a low price for the extra product, but it is extra food that they would not normally have purchased, so they fail to save money in the long run.

Michael Fumento, *The Fat of the Land: The Obesity Epidemic and How Overweight Americans Can Help Themselves.* New York: Viking, 1997, p. 44.

Yet the more a food is processed, the more fiber is taken out of it, and the more calories are added in its place. A pound of unpeeled potatoes, for example, has only 289 calories. When that same pound of potatoes is fried in oil and processed into potato chips, it has 2,400 calories. Nutritionist and author Marion Nestle says it is ironic that people in less-developed nations of the world tend to eat a healthier, higher-fiber diet than Americans, because they cannot afford or do not have access to processed foods like potato chips. Only as people become better off, she says, do they "abandon traditional plant-based diets and begin eating more meat, fat, and processed foods. The result is a sharp increase in obesity and related chronic diseases."[10]

Supersize Portions

Not only are Americans eating more processed foods, they are also eating more of everything else. A frequently cited reason for rising rates of obesity in the United States is the tremendous increase in portion sizes over the past few decades. Family restaurants serve up plates heaped full of food. Supermarkets and warehouse stores sell large value packs of cookies, giant boxes of cereals, and huge bricks of cheese. Food chains compete to offer the biggest meals: Burger King's Triple Whopper hamburger contains three beef patties, while Denny's Super Slam breakfast boasts three eggs, three pancakes, three sausage links, and three strips of bacon. Nutritionists caution that there

Supersized fast food provides a huge hit of fat, calories, and sodium but little that is of nutritional value.

is no longer any correlation between the size of the portions being offered and the amount of food people need to maintain healthy diets and weights.

The trend toward inflated portions in the United States is driven by the fast-food industry. In the 1970s, corporate officials at McDonald's discovered that they could boost sales by offering much larger portions at only slightly higher prices. The company still made a profit, because doubling the size of a cup of soda or a bag of fries added very little to its costs. And sales went up as more people were drawn to the restaurants to take advantage of the large-size bargains. All the major fast-food chains soon began increasing container sizes and promoting the added value of the new supersize meals. They used terms like, *jumbo*, *macho* meal, and *monster* to appeal to the American view that bigger is better.

The products that the fast-food chains are most likely to supersize are often loaded with fat, calories, and sodium and are

low in vitamins, fiber, and other nutrients. "You're getting extra french fries, more soft drink, cheap stuff that is essentially filler," says nutrition expert Adam Drewenowski. "No one is offering you a large salad for the price of a small one."[11]

Among the new jumbo meals introduced in recent years, for example, is Hardee's Monster Thickburger hamburger, a 1,410-calorie sandwich that is the equivalent of two McDonald's Big Mac hamburgers. This monster burger is marketed as the only thing "that can slay the hunger of a young guy on the move."[12] When it is combined with a medium serving of Hardee's fries, the meal contains more calories and fat than are recommended for most people to eat in an entire day.

Soda and Sweetened Beverages

In addition to eating more food Americans are also drinking more. Over the past fifty years, they have begun to consume huge amounts of soda, juice drinks, beer, other alcoholic beverages, and sweetened coffees. The leading source of calories in the American diet was once white bread, but researchers report that Americans today are drinking their calories instead. More than two-thirds of respondents on a 1999–2000 national health survey said that they consumed enough soda and other sweetened drinks to provide a greater proportion of their total calories than any other food.

Soda sales in the United States are huge—about the same as the market value of all goods and services produced in a country the size of Ireland or New Zealand. A few large and highly influential companies control most of these sales. The two biggest, Coca-Cola and PepsiCo, sell 70 percent of the carbonated beverages in the world. These companies spend hundreds of millions of dollars to market their products through TV commercials, billboards, the Internet, radio, and sponsorship of high-profile concerts, sporting events, and cultural activities. Throughout the world, the Coke and Pepsi brand names are associated with American life and popular culture.

Yet the products these companies market so effectively contain no nutritional value. Soda is made with water, sugar or other sweeteners such as high fructose corn syrup, caffeine, salt, and chemicals. Nutritionists sometimes refer to soda as "liquid candy," because it has become the leading source of sugar in the American diet. There are roughly ten teaspoons of sugar or other caloric sweeteners in a 12-ounce (.35L) can of soda, just two teaspoons short of the maximum allotment the government recommends that Americans ingest in an entire day.

The portion sizes of soda and other high-calorie beverages have also grown enormously along with the meals they accompany. At fast-food chains, coffee stores, and restaurants, a small cup has ballooned to the size that was once a medium, a medium has become a large, and the large has become gigantic. Customers who order a small soda at Wendy's, for example, get a cup filled with 16 ounces (.47L) of liquid. Customers with a harder-to-quench thirst who order a Biggie Soda get a full quart (.95L). Automakers have been forced to widen car cup holders to make room for the larger 12-ounce (.35L) bottles of soda sold in supermarkets today. But the new cup holders are still not equipped to handle the largest of the supersize drinks. These include the 52-ounce (1.5L) XTreme Gulp, sold at 7-Eleven convenience stores, and the Beast, available at ARCO gas stations. The Beast is a refillable monster-size cup containing a seemingly bottomless 85 ounces (2.5L) of soda.

Changing American Eating Habits and Culture

Fast-food chains such as McDonald's and Wendy's promote soda as part of their supersize meals and sell a huge volume of it each day. Yet increased soda consumption is only one of the ways in which the fast-food industry has changed Americans' eating habits and lifestyles. The mass appeal and affordability of fast-food restaurants allow people of all income levels to eat out more and cook less. Americans take this for granted today, but there was a time when dining out was a luxury that few people could afford. The change is usually credited to the vision of two brothers, Richard and Maurice McDonald, who opened the first McDonald's restaurant in San Bernardino, California, in 1948. The brothers put into place a revolutionary system of food preparation and service that they called the Speedee Service System.

Schlosser recounts that they increased efficiency and sales volume by offering a limited number of menu items, eliminating foods that required a knife or fork, and replacing glasses and dishware with paper goods. They also divided food preparation into separate tasks, assembly line-style, so that one employee spread the sauce and another wrapped the burgers in paper.

BUSES AND GROCERY CARTS

"Many urban community dwellers would love to have better eating habits, but if there's no grocery store nearby, you're talking about getting on public transportation with a grocery cart."

Maya Rockeymoore of the National Urban League quoted in Kelly D. Brownell and Katherine Battle Horgen, *Food Fight: The Inside Story of the Food Industry, America's Obesity Crisis, & What We Can Do About It.* Chicago: McGraw-Hill Contemporary Books, 2004, p. 40.

McDonald's pioneer Ray Kroc took the McDonald's Speedee Service concept to cities, suburbs, and highway exits across the nation. He created a huge chain of clean, efficient restaurants that made eating out affordable and convenient for working-class Americans and their families for the first time. Other early fast-food pioneers followed his lead. Burger King, Kentucky Fried Chicken, Carl's Jr., Wendy's, and other chains began to open franchises across the nation throughout the 1960s and early 1970s.

Today the major fast-food chains have become a familiar part of the American landscape. It is estimated that roughly a quarter of the adult population and a third of children and teens in the United States visit a fast-food restaurant on any given day. In just thirty years, from the 1970s to 2001, U.S. spending on fast food expanded from $6 billion to more than $110 billion per year.

Yet health advocates say the tremendous popularity of fast food is a major contributor to weight gain and related illness. The all-American meals served at most fast-food restaurants are extremely high in calories, fat, and sodium. In his 2004 documentary film, *Super Size Me*, filmmaker Morgan Spurlock put himself on a McDonald's-only, no-exercise diet for thirty consecutive days as a social experiment aimed at exposing the fast-food industry's role in promoting obesity. He subsisted on hamburgers, fries, and soda, ordered the supersize portions whenever he was asked by a McDonald's employee if he wanted to size up, and sampled every item on the menu at least once. At the end of the thirty days, he had gained 24.5 pounds (11.1kg)—almost a pound a day—and suffered from rising cholesterol levels, an inflamed liver, and heart palpitations. Food-industry groups argued that few people would eat this much fast food in a single month. Yet although his diet was extreme, even Spurlock's doctors were surprised by the extent to which it had caused his health to deteriorate.

Sedentary Lifestyles

Despite the popularity of fast food, Americans might not be gaining so much weight if they were not also burning off fewer calo-

Filmmaker Morgan Spurlock, who ate nothing but McDonald's food for a month, poses with the poster for his movie about the debilitating experience.

ries in physical activity than ever before. Some people argue that obesity studies focus too heavily on overeating as a cause of weight gain and ignore the equally important role played by inactivity. The United States has become one of the most sedentary cultures in the world. Simply put: Americans are not burning enough calories or staying active enough to maintain good health.

FAST FOOD

"Fast food is terrible for you. It shouldn't even be called 'food.' It should be called more like what it is: a highly efficient delivery system for fats, carbohydrates, sugars and other bad things."

Morgan Spurlock, *Don't Eat This Book: Fast Food and the Supersizing of America*. New York: G.P. Putnam's Sons, 2005, p. 24.

Most health experts recommend that people get at least thirty minutes of moderate-intensity physical activity five days a week. Children are advised to get at least one hour of physical activity each day. "Moderate can mean walking slowly enough to maintain a normal conversation. Yet a recent CDC study found that more than half of American adults fail to achieve even this minimum amount of physical activity. Fifteen percent of adults are almost completely sedentary. They perform almost no active housework, rarely walk, and spend their leisure time sitting still.

One of the main obstacles to physical exertion is the time Americans spend sitting in their cars. The United States is a huge country, with cities and suburbs that sprawl over vast areas. Americans drive more and walk less than people in almost any other nation in the world. They commute long distances to work and drive to school, to shopping malls, and to run errands in their own communities. In many residential areas, sidewalks are rare. Shopping centers are often islands of concrete surrounded by busy roads and highways that are dangerous to cross by foot. Many workplaces are inaccessible by public transport. With Americans driving everywhere, the nation's roads and highway systems have become more jammed than ever. The time that people spend sitting in their cars, stalled in traffic, jumped a staggering 236 percent in a decade, from the mid-1980s to the mid-1990s.

Home and work lives have also become more sedentary. Americans are quick to embrace almost any new technology that saves them time and energy. Housework once involved tremendous physical exertion—from scrubbing clothes by hand on a washboard to cleaning the oven with a scouring pad. Today people use remote control devices to operate their televisions, stereos, and garage doors. They set the oven to self-clean and let the dishwasher scrub the pots and pans. They also increasingly spend their leisure time watching television and DVDs, surfing the Web, playing video games, and instant messaging their friends.

INEXPENSIVE AND HEALTHY

"I think cost is not a determiner of whether or not you eat properly. I mean, there's fruits and vegetables out there, a lot of inexpensive foods that can be extremely healthy. . . . There's a lot that you can do with a budget from a low-income person that can be very healthy."

Tommy G. Thompson, Secretary of the U.S. Department of Health and Human Services quoted in U.S. Department of Health and Human Services, "Transcript of HHS and USDA Press Conference Announcement of New DietaryGuidelines for Americans," January 12, 2005. www.health.gov/dietaryguidelines/dga2005/transcript.

Computers and other labor-saving devices have also transformed the American workplace. The U.S. economy today is centered on desk jobs that require little physical exertion. People are able to make phone calls, send e-mails, search reference books on the Internet, and read newspaper and magazine articles, all without getting up from their swivel chairs.

Genes Versus Environment

This trend toward a more sedentary lifestyle at work and home affects Americans of every income level and racial group. People of all backgrounds are eating more and exercising less. Although they have all inherited the same basic human biology, some people remain thin while others become obese. Scientists believe genetic factors may play a role. A child with severely overweight parents has a high likelihood of becoming overweight too. Studies also show that the BMIs of adopted children tend to match more closely to those of their biological parents than those of their adoptive parents.

Genetic factors alone, however, cannot account for the rapid rise of weight gain and obesity in the United States. The human gene pool changes very gradually, over thousands of years. Obesity rates in the United States have nearly doubled in less than thirty years. Scientists suggest that when people who are genetically prone to weight gain are exposed to environmental conditions in which high-calorie foods are plentiful—as they are in the United States today—they are more likely to become obese. "Biology is important," say Brownell and Battle Horgen, "but the environment steals the show."[13]

Immigrants and Obesity

In one of New York City's Chinese neighborhoods, recent immigrants flock to traditional markets to buy poultry, Chinese cabbage, bean sprouts, and other fresh vegetables. They sip from bowls of steaming broth at nearby noodle shops and prepare traditional meals at home for their families. Their children, however, frequently reject these foods in favor of hamburgers, soda, pizza, and candy. "At home we would shop in the open market," Jian Kang Qiu, a forty-three-year-old immigrant from China's Guangdong province told a *New York Times* reporter. "There was not so much packaged food. We would eat maybe two meals a day. Rice with something on the side, fish or vegetables." But after just six years in the United States, Qiu and his family are eating a diet high in fat, processed sugar, and sodium. Qiu's mother and sister have been diagnosed with type 2 diabetes. (Asian immigrants are susceptible to type 2 diabetes at lower weights than most other racial groups.) And Qiu has given up trying to control what his teenage daughter eats. "She would prefer American food," he says. "Her friends are going for pizza, she wants to go for pizza."

Quoted in Marc Santora, "East Meets West, Adding Pounds and Peril," *New York Times*, January 12, 2006, National Desk, p. 1.

Some of the most compelling evidence that obesity is closely tied to environment comes from the experience of immigrant groups living in the United States. A large-scale study of more than thirty-two thousand people who responded to a national health survey, 14 percent of them immigrants, found that obesity is relatively rare in the foreign born until they have lived in the United States for more than ten years. Only 8 percent of immigrants who had lived in the country for less than a year were obese, but that jumped to 19 percent among those who had lived in the country for at least fifteen years. Even researchers who suspected that people would gain weight as they adopted the eating habits and lifestyles of their new country were surprised by the magnitude of the change. "The very act of living in the United States," says *The Fat of the Land* author Michael Fumento, "puts you at greater risk for obesity."[14]

EATING HABITS AND LIFESTYLE AMONG AMERICAN YOUTH

For children and teenagers in the United States, the cultural and social forces that promote weight gain and obesity are especially powerful. At schools, shopping malls, movie theaters, stadiums, and amusement parks—almost everywhere that young people spend their time—they are surrounded by inducements to eat high-calorie foods. They are the targets of multibillion-dollar advertising campaigns designed to persuade them that one brand of snack food or soda is better than another. Often their favorite TV characters, sports heroes, and music stars endorse these food products. When they eat at restaurants, they choose from kids' menus that offer fat-laden meals such as chicken fingers, french fries, cheeseburgers, and pizza. Even their toddler counting books show pictures of M&M's candies and Hershey's Kisses chocolate.

At the same time that they are eating more, children and teenagers are also burning fewer calories. Television, movies, video games, and computers vie for their attention and keep them sitting still for hours at a time. In many communities they have little time for informal, active play and are driven to school, activities, and playdates. The result is that the majority of U.S. children fail to meet the exercise and dietary guidelines recommended by the USDA to grow and maintain healthy bodies.

Weighing in on Young People

The rate of overweight in children of all races, ages, and genders in the United States is climbing rapidly. Until the 1960s,

Teens eat high-calorie buttered popcorn and drink sugary sodas during a sedentary afternoon at the movies.

that rate remained steady at around 5 or 6 percent of young people, but by the year 2000, 16 percent—roughly 9 million U.S. children—were estimated to be overweight. Another 15 percent of children were considered at risk for becoming overweight. The average ten-year-old boy or girl in the United States today weighs approximately eleven pounds more than a child the same age in the 1970s. The percentage of overweight children of African American, Native American, and Mexican American descent, and those of lower income, is significantly higher than that of middle- and upper-income white children.

Health officials say the rising percentage of overweight children is deeply troubling, but that it is also important to keep the numbers in perspective. The vast majority of children still fall in the normal weight range. Even among young children who are overweight, there may not be cause for concern. Long-term studies suggest that most overweight five- or seven-year-olds do not become obese adults.

Yet for children who are severely overweight or those who are overweight as adolescents, the health risks are serious and even life threatening. Most of the severely obese adults in the country were first overweight as teenagers. This is especially true for women. Extremely overweight children and teens are at great risk for health problems such as high blood pressure, heart disease,

Overweight teens face a tough battle to keep their weight under control.

asthma, and obstructive sleep apnea, a dangerous condition in which they experience interrupted breathing during sleep. In the largest study of children's health of its kind in the world, researchers at Tulane University tracked thousands of children in the racially mixed, semirural community of Bogalusa, Louisiana. They looked for early warning signs of heart disease and high blood pressure and discovered that more than 60 percent of overweight children between five and ten years old had already developed at least one risk factor for heart disease.

Overweight children also have a higher risk of type 2 diabetes. For decades doctors believed that type 2 diabetes, once called adult-onset diabetes, was a disease of aging that progressed gradually as the cells of the body became less sensitive to insulin. But that changed with the rise of childhood obesity, as more children began arriving at hospitals and clinics with alarmingly high blood sugar levels. A genetic predisposition to diabetes tends to run in families, but the disease is clearly linked to excess weight and a lack of physical activity. It is estimated that one out of every three American children born in the year 2000 will get the disease at some time in their lives. For poor and minority children, the risk is even greater.

What Children Are Eating

Scientists believe that obesity-related diseases such as type 2 diabetes are occurring frequently in childhood today primarily because young people in the United States are consuming so much high-calorie, sugary, and fat-laden junk food. The USDA guidelines advise that children eat a balanced diet heavy in nutrient-dense foods and beverages from each of the five food groups, which include grains, vegetables, fruits, milk, and meat and beans. Most children, however, fall far short of meeting these guidelines. For example, the guidelines recommend that children consume at least five servings (roughly 2 1/2 cups) of fruits and vegetables per day. Yet the average school-age child in the United States eats closer to just 1/2 cup of fruit and only 1/4 cup of vegetables. And of the vegetables children do consume, almost a quarter take the form of potato chips or french fries, while almost half of the fruit comes from sweetened fruit juice.

When poor children's diets are evaluated, researchers find that their eating habits are even worse.

The problem is that although potato chips, sweetened fruit juice, and other processed and packaged foods supply the calories children need to grow and develop, they lack vital nutrients. They are also loaded with sugar and so-called bad (saturated or trans) fats. The World Health Organization advises that people completely eliminate processed sugar from their diet, but Americans often feed processed sugar to their babies and young children. A jar of Heinz custard pudding baby food, for example, contains nearly four teaspoons of sugar, roughly the amount that can be found in the same size serving of soda. Breakfast cereals that are marketed to very young children are rolled, coated, and dipped in processed sugar. Even parents who try to keep sugary and salty junk foods out of the hands of their young children are forced to fight the nation's food culture. "Parents must compete with television, movies, candy fundraisers, schools filled with soft drinks, snack foods, and fast foods, and peer pressure to eat,"[15] say Brownell and Battle Horgen.

TRASH FOOD

"The nation has not yet had the courage to stand up against trash food and has forgotten how to send our kids out to play. The bodies of our young are becoming trash and there is no time to play."

Derrick Z. Jackson, "Diabetes and the Trash Food Industry," *Boston Globe*, January 11, 2006, p. A15.

As children grow older and enter school, their eating habits become worse. School-age kids pack potato chips, crackers, cheese puffs, sugar-laden yogurt, muffins, and candy for lunch and snacks. They also consume several servings of sweetened beverages such as soda, chocolate milk, or artificial fruit drinks each day. They snack on chips and pretzels at baseball and soccer games and celebrate victory with their teammates at Pizza Hut and McDonald's.

American teenagers consume many of the same unhealthy processed and packaged foods as younger children, but in much larger amounts. They eat few servings of fruits or green vegetables and purchase many of their meals away from home, often at fast-food chains. They also guzzle huge amounts of soda and sweetened fruit drinks. According to a report by the nonprofit nutrition and health advocacy group Center for Science in the Public Interest (CSPI), the average teenage boy drinks two cans of soda a day, almost triple the amount consumed twenty years ago. Teenage boys get an estimated 13 percent of their daily calories from soda and noncarbonated fruit drinks, while teenage girls, among the most poorly nourished of any group in the United States, reportedly get 10 to 15 percent of their daily calories from soft drinks.

American children of all ages also eat out more frequently than in the past at fast-food chains and family-style restaurants,

where they are served up not only soda but also nearly double the food calories that they would normally consume at home. CSPI surveyed twenty of America's biggest table-service restaurants that offer kids' menus, including. Applebee's, Outback Steakhouse, and Chili's, and found that most featured oversize portions of burgers, fries, and deep-fried chicken fingers. All these menu items were exceedingly high in calories and fat. CSPI reported, for example, that the cheeseburger with fries from the kids' menu at Outback Steakhouse contains the same number of calories as an adult order of sirloin steak and filet mignon combined, plus three pats of butter.

UNDERMINED BY ADS

"Parents' choices about their children's eating habits are undermined by junk food ads everyday. Although parents may want their kids to eat healthy, they often lose out because Sponge Bob Square Pants, Shrek, and cartoon superheroes entice kids to eat fast food and sugary snacks."

Senator Tom Harkin, quoted in Harkin.senate.gov, "Harkin Calls on Food Industry to Limit Junk Food Advertising Aimed at Kids," March 16, 2005. www.harkin.senate.gov/news.cfm?id=233655.

Marketing Food to Children Is Big Business

The decline in quality of children's eating habits in the United States comes at a time when there is a huge increase in food marketing aimed directly at children and teens. On TV, the Internet, billboards, and vending machines and in supermarkets and toy stores—almost everywhere that children turn—they are exposed to ads for high-calorie foods. The food industry spends more than $12 billion each year on marketing aimed at persuading U.S. children to consume more food products. They hire consultants who specialize in devising clever new ways to give these products maximum kid appeal. For food companies looking to boost their profits, children represent a winning combination. They not only exert tremendous influence over their families' food purchases, but they are also easily persuaded by

Bruce Willis appears on MTV with VJ Vanessa Minnillo. Food companies market their products intensively on channels like MTV that attract youthful audiences.

advertising. "The aim of most children's advertising is straight-forward: get kids to nag their parents and nag them well,"[16] explains *Fast Food Nation* author Schlosser.

The food marketing assault in the United States begins early in childhood. Market research has shown that a single thirty-second advertisement can promote brand loyalty in children as young as age two. Repeated exposure to an ad is even more effective. Marketers appeal directly to very young children in their ads and packaging with colorful graphics and familiar characters. Juice companies such as Motts and Libby's, for example, feature *Sesame Street*, *Arthur*, and *Rugrats* characters on boxes of fruit juice. Toys and books, such as Coca-Cola Barbies and plastic McDonald's food carts, also help to constantly remind young children of their favorite food products.

Despite the growing importance of the Internet and other new technologies, television remains the medium of choice for most food marketers. Commercials for food products flood the airwaves of cable television networks that cater to children and teens, such as Nickelodeon, MTV, and the Cartoon Network. Kids who watch television on Saturday morning are bombarded with roughly one food commercial every five minutes. Four out of five of these ads are for sugary cereals, snack foods, candy, soft drinks, and fast food. Yet the food industry's marketing goes far beyond conventional TV commercials. Most of the shows and movies children watch are linked to off-screen food promotions. These marketing tie-ins lure children to choose foods connected to their favorite movie or TV characters. As a result, supermarket shelves are loaded with products such as Rugrats Macaroni and Cheese, Scooby Doo Lunchable lunches, Big Bird animal crackers, and Pokémon fruit roll ups.

JUST SAY NO

"We want kids to buy our products. But Mom and Dad, if your kid is eating too much and eating the wrong stuff, don't let them have it."

Steven Rotter, food marketer quoted in Nat Ives, "The Media Business: Advertising; A Report the Possibility That Ads Contribute to Obesity in Children; the Industry Begs to Differ," *New York Times*, February 25, 2004, Business Section, p. 3.

One of the hottest marketing trends in recent years is for companies to emphasize fun in their ads. They promote foods with bright colors, unusual forms and shapes, and innovative packaging. Marketers call this phenomenon eatertainment. Food products that fit this category include fruit snacks that kids punch out to make Nickelodeon characters, purple ketchup, and even french fries that are available in five flavors, including cinnamon and sugar and chocolate. "Food commercials aimed at children don't talk as much about 'great taste' as they do about having fun—associating food with action, friends, excitement," says Susan Linn, author of *Consuming Kids*, "None of these are good reasons for eating."[17]

Ways the Fast-Food Industry Markets to Youth

Fast-food companies also aggressively target children in their marketing. McDonald's pioneer Kroc recognized early that children were desirable customers because they usually brought parents and grandparents along with them when they visited a restaurant. The average bill for a family is three times that of a nonfamily transaction, so the major fast-food chains work hard to make their restaurants attractive, safe, all-American places for parents and kids.

McDonald's and Disney Create Marketing Synergy

In 1997, the Disney Company signed a ten-year deal with McDonald's that gave the fast-food chain exclusive rights to distribute certain products related to the studio's output of films and videos. Marketers call this kind of arrangement "synergy," since each company helps to promote the other. McDonald's capitalized on the release of new Disney movies by giving away Disney action figures with its Happy Meals, and Disney received publicity for the new movies every time a child visited a McDonald's restaurant. Many children begged their parents to make repeat visits to McDonald's until they had collected every toy in a series.

With the Disney deal expiring, McDonald's has negotiated similar agreements with other studios, including DreamWorks. The new deals, however, will go beyond toy promotions in an effort to attract kids to the restaurants. Ronald McDonald will appear with popular DreamWorks characters in the chain's ads, for example. Other fast-food chains including Burger King, Taco Bell, and Wendy's have also negotiated for the rights to distribute toys linked to popular kids' movies and shows—from *Pokémon* to *Star Wars*.

A McDonald's executive displays a small pile of the 2.4 million Teenie Beanie Babies that the chain used to market its food to young people in 1997.

There are fast-food restaurants in almost every community where children live, travel, and attend school. A recent study in Chicago found that children in nearly all the schools in the city are only a ten-minute walk from at least one fast-food chain. There are fast-food franchises at stadiums, cineplexes, suburban minimalls, even children's hospitals. Still, companies such as McDonald's and Burger King do not leave anything to chance. They spend millions of dollars on advertising to ensure that young people walk through their doors.

Fast-food companies aggressively court children in other ways too. McDonald's operates close to eight thousand playgrounds, more than any other private company in the United States. Burger King has more than two thousand U.S. playgrounds.

These colorful play spaces are highly effective in attracting families with young children. In some low-income, inner-city neighborhoods where there are few clean, safe public parks or playgrounds, McDonaldland may be the only place where parents feel comfortable bringing young children to play.

Fast-food companies also entice children with toys and characters linked to their favorite movies, TV shows, and sports teams. McDonald's is one of the largest toy distributors in the nation. A popular toy promotion can easily double or even triple weekly sales of the company's children's meals. In 1997, for example, McDonald's launched the Teenie Beanie Baby campaign, one of the most successful marketing efforts in U.S. advertising history. At the time, McDonald's normally sold about 10 million Happy Meals per week. During ten days in April 1997, when the chain included a Teenie Beanie Baby with each purchase, sales skyrocketed to 100 million Happy Meals.

When measured by the number of U.S. children who regularly eat at a fast-food restaurant, these marketing strategies are a resounding success. On a typical day, a third of U.S. children consume a fast-food meal. Every month, more than three-quarters of American children between the ages of three and nine visit a McDonald's restaurant. Yet the children's meals at these restaurants are loaded with fat, sodium, sugar, and calories. "They [fast-food chains] don't think about nutrition if it interferes with profits,"[18] says *Diabesity* author Kaufman.

A Decline in Physical Fitness

At the same time that U.S. children are indulging in more snacks and fast foods, they are also exerting themselves less. The evidence is overwhelming that when inactivity is combined with diets high in fat and sugar, the risk of obesity grows. Yet children and teens in the United States today belong to the most sedentary generation in history.

Some health experts blame television for children's lack of physical fitness. American children spend more time watching television than doing anything else except sleeping. Children who view excessive amounts of TV tend to engage in active play less than their peers who watch fewer hours of television. (Some studies, however, suggest that teens who are not watching might still be inactive, playing video games, talking on cell phones, or reading.) They are also exposed to hundreds of TV ads that prompt them to snack while they watch. A landmark 1985 study found a strong link between the number of hours of television a child watched and the risk of becoming overweight or obese. More recent studies have confirmed that as much as 60 percent of the incidence of overweight in children ages ten to fifteen can be associated with TV viewing in excess of four or five hours a day. Add to that time spent logged onto the Internet, playing video and computer games, instant messaging friends, and using handheld games, and it is clear that U.S. children are burning fewer calories than ever before.

The Social Stigma of Obesity: One Teenager's Story

Obese teenagers often suffer from anxiety and depression. They may feel isolated and hopeless and blame themselves for failing to lose weight. A severely obese seventeen-year-old girl from Rochester, New York, related her story on the American Obesity Association Web site:

> I've been overweight since I was 12 years old. I used to go to school, but I had to drop out because people continued to make fun of me.
>
> I suffer from depression, anxiety and agoraphobia [fear of public spaces]. I hate my body so much and I wish I could lose all this weight in a heartbeat, but I can't.
>
> Now I sit around in the house all day, and when I do go out I don't even get out of the car. I joined a gym, but I don't know what good that's going to do.
>
> I missed my whole teenage-hood because of my obesity. . . . I feel so guilty for letting myself get so big and I wish I could just live an ordinary teenage life. . . . I really need some support right now. I wish all these pretty skinny, in-shape people could just respect me, but that will never happen because of the way I look.

American Obesity Association, "My Story #6," www. obesity.org/subs/story/entirestorys.shtml.

Physical activity is on a downward slide for other reasons too. Children in the United States walk and ride their bikes far less than in previous decades. The National Transportation Board estimates that roughly 66 percent of children in the 1970s walked or biked to school. Today that number has fallen to just 10 percent. In many suburbs, schools are out of walking range or located across busy streets and highways. Parents are reluctant to let children walk because they fear for their safety. The problem is worse in many low-income communities with high crime rates, where it is sometimes dangerous for children to be out on the streets at certain hours of the day. In many of these same communities, parks and playgrounds have fallen into disrepair or are considered unsafe for play.

Even the country's growing number of youth soccer, baseball, hockey, tennis, gymnastics, and other organized sports leagues are out of reach for many American children. These have replaced casual play and pickup games in many places, but they are expensive to start and maintain and require heavy parent involvement. They also tend to become highly competitive as children grow older. As a result, children who are less confident about their athletic abilities are likely to drop out of these leagues by their teenage years and are left with few other outlets for physical activity. Many children do not exercise at all by the time they reach age eighteen or nineteen.

This trend toward sedentary living is even worse for girls than for boys. American popular culture stresses appearance, thinness, and glamour for girls, rather than athletic skill, fitness, or overall health. When the media do focus on girls in sports, the messages are often confusing. Stories about female athletes tend to emphasize appearance or femininity rather than athleticism. The result is that by age fifteen, many girls in the United States lead almost entirely sedentary lives.

Schools Play a Role in Children's Weight Gain

Many children and teens are not exercising at school either. Because schools are often crowded, in need of money, and under pressure to improve academic standards and test scores, physical fitness has become a low priority. In fact many school sys-

High school seniors lunch on fatty pizza and hamburgers in their school cafeteria.

tems have abandoned the requirement for physical education (PE) altogether. A survey by the CDC found that the percentage of U.S. students who attended daily PE classes in high school dropped from 42 percent in 1991 to 28 percent in 2003. The percentages were even lower in mainly African American and Latino school districts, which often lack the money and resources to keep PE programs going. Even when schools do offer traditional gym classes, they tend to favor children who are the most athletic and coordinated. Kids who are overweight or less coordinated than their peers often end up on the sidelines. "If you're a bit clumsy, a bit uncoordinated, a bit self-conscious— you're left out,"[19]says Reginald Washington, cochair of a national task force on obesity.

Schools are also among the worst offenders when it comes to providing children with access to high-calorie snack and junk foods. Cafeteria lunches often include chicken nuggets, pizza, cheeseburgers, and hot dogs. These are washed down with sweetened drinks such as soda, fruit punch, or strawberry and chocolate milk. Many schools sell soda, candy, and high-calorie snack foods in vending machines, school stores, and a la carte lines in the cafeteria. Others allow fast-food franchises such as Subway, Taco Bell, and Pizza Hut to operate right on campus.

Schools sell junk food and soda in vending machines and cafeterias because this is a guaranteed way to earn money. These sales are especially appealing to officials in low-income school districts who often rely on the profits to purchase computers, sports equipment, art supplies, and other expensive items. Many schools also enter into exclusive "pouring rights" contracts with soda companies. They agree to sell the company's products exclusively in exchange for a signing bonus and a share of profits. They are then obligated to sell and promote the company's brand on vending machines, scoreboards and stadium banners, and in hallways. One government report found that nearly half of all U.S. schools had pouring rights contracts with a beverage company in the 2003–2004 school year. (In 2005, the American Beverage Association, with backing from Coke and Pepsi, attempted to head off bad publicity about these deals by voluntarily refusing to sell carbonated drinks in elementary schools.)

The result is that schools have become accomplices in the growing epidemic of childhood obesity. When health experts consider what schools are teaching children about diet and lifestyle, they see a missed opportunity. "Childhood," says Kaufman, "is when youngsters begin to develop the habits that will be with them for a lifetime. This is the time to teach them about the benefits of good nutrition and physical activity."[20]

THE ROLE OF THE FOOD INDUSTRY

Health advocates have begun to demand that food manufacturers, restaurants, and fast-food chains—among them some of the largest, most profitable companies in the world—be held accountable for rising rates of obesity among U.S. children and adults. Companies such as McDonald's, Burger King, Coca-Cola, Kraft Foods, General Mills, and Kellogg's have tremendous political power and influence in American society. Health groups accuse these companies of ignoring medical advice about the dangers of overeating high-calorie foods and encouraging people to consume foods that are bad for their health. They do this by spending millions of dollars on advertising, packaging food in oversize portions, and targeting their marketing at vulnerable groups such as children and the poor. In recent years support has been growing for measures to crack down on food-industry practices such as advertising to young children and selling junk food in schools, which are seen as major contributors to the nation's obesity epidemic.

Food-industry groups argue that attempts to police the sale of food and soda are misguided. The United States is a free-market economy, they say, and consumers must take responsibility for their own food choices. Although some food companies have been persuaded in the face of increasing public and media scrutiny to introduce healthier menu options and limit the food products they advertise to children, critics say these steps rarely go far enough. With Americans' long-term health at stake, they believe that society must intervene to make fundamental changes in the way the food industry does business.

Taming Big Food: The Example of the Tobacco Industry

Health advocates often cite the nation's successful campaign against cigarette smoking as a model of how to battle the powerful food and soda industries. In the 1980s and 1990s, the government sponsored a series of high-profile public service announcements that linked smoking to lung cancer and premature death and gave cigarettes a reputation as "death sticks." Many cities and states raised taxes on cigarettes and enacted sweeping new laws banning smoking in restaurants, bars, and public buildings. The major tobacco companies, collectively known as Big Tobacco, were pressured into accepting restrictions on advertising their products. They were also forced to pay enormous legal settlements for knowingly concealing the dangers of their products for decades and causing long-time smokers to become sick with lung cancer and other ailments.

Health and nutrition groups contend that there are many parallels between Big Tobacco and Big Food. They say that like cigarette companies, food and soda manufacturers have used misleading and aggressive advertising and other deceitful tactics

Teens sip drinks bought from machines at their high school. Pressure is growing to remove sugary drinks and unhealthy foods from schools.

to encourage people to consume products that are bad for their health. Snack products that are marketed as low fat, for example, are often high in calories and still contribute to weight gain, just as cigarettes sold as lite or low tar can still cause addiction. Critics even compare Ronald McDonald, a figure recognized by more U.S. schoolchildren (96 percent) than any other fictional character except Santa Claus, to the former Camel cigarette mascot, Joe Camel. This hip cartoon character appealed to young people and was believed to encourage them to try smoking. In some cases the ties between the tobacco and food industries go even deeper than the use of similar marketing tactics. Companies such as Planters, Oscar Mayer, and Nabisco are owned by Kraft Foods, the largest food company in the world, which in turn is owned by tobacco giant Philip Morris.

CONSPIRACIES

"Like Big Tobacco, it [Big Food] characterizes critics as a conspiracy of 'food cops,' health care enforcers, vegetarian activists and meddling bureaucrats. . . . Like Big Tobacco, it makes us believe that our freedom of choice depends on its freedom to garner profits."

Ellen Ruppel Shell, *The Hungry Gene: The Science of Fat and The Future of Thin.* New York: Atlantic Monthly, 2002, p. 230.

Yet there are also many ways in which tobacco and food are different, and this may make it harder to place the blame on the food industry for rising rates of obesity. Food is critical for human survival, while smoking has no accepted health value and is not necessary to live. Selling cigarettes to minors is against the law, but selling food to them is not. The tobacco industry is dominated by a handful of companies that collectively manufacture a product that is known to be harmful and addictive. In contrast, hundreds of food companies sell and produce many thousands of different packaged and processed snacks, desserts, cereals, dairy products, meats, and beverages. It is hard to prove that they are deliberately concealing the health risks of

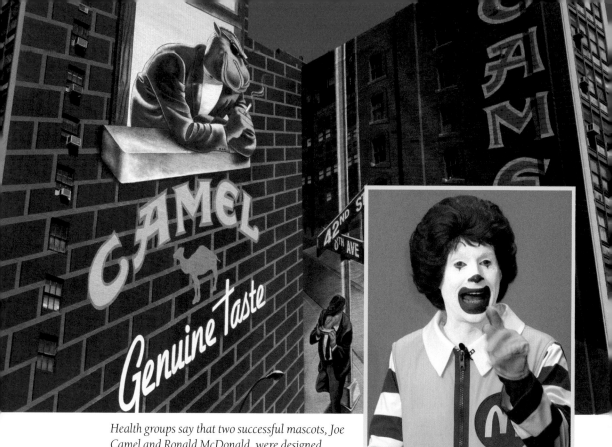

Health groups say that two successful mascots, Joe Camel and Ronald McDonald, were designed to appeal to young people.

their products or trying to promote overeating. And although scientists believe that a few fatty foods, chocolate, and sugar may have addictive properties that cause changes in behavior and brain chemistry similar to those experienced by tobacco smokers, the evidence for this is inconclusive. As a result the American public has been reluctant to equate smoking with overeating or to apply the same strategies used against the tobacco industry to wage war against Big Food.

Restrictions on Food Marketing to Children

Health advocates believe they have the greatest chance of mobilizing public support to reform the food industry by first addressing issues such as marketing to children and junk-food sales in schools. Polls show that Americans are troubled by the unhealthy food environment that surrounds children from a very young age. They are disturbed by reports of U.S. children suffering from type 2 diabetes and high blood pressure. Even those who insist that obesity and weight gain among adults should be a matter of personal responsibility often blame the food industry for exploiting children who are too young to make decisions about their long-term health.

With public support increasingly on their side, health groups and a growing number of state and federal lawmakers have begun to demand action to protect children from junk-food advertising. Some have proposed banning TV commercials for food during the hours when children are most likely to be watching. Others insist that equal time be allotted on TV networks for the promotion of healthy foods such as fruits and vegetables, paid for with food-industry money. (In the 1970s, the government threatened to force cigarette manufacturers to give equal time to antitobacco ads, and this led to an industry-wide agreement to end all TV advertising of cigarettes.) Yet many child advocacy groups say that the proposed measures do not go far enough. They insist that nothing short of a total ban on children's food advertising is likely to be effective.

FOOD DOES NOT KILL

"Cigarettes are one of those products that, when used as directed, will kill you. I don't believe there is much food out there that, when eaten responsibly, is going to kill you."

Quoted in Kate Zernike, "The Nation: Food Fight; Is Obesity the Responsibility of the Body Politic?" *New York Times*, November 9, 2003, Week in Review, p. 3.

Public support is also growing for measures to ban the sale of soda and junk food in schools. Food and beverage sales on school campuses represent only a tiny fraction of total industry sales worldwide, but they are of great value to food companies who hope to influence children's buying habits and create loyal customers for life. In recent years, opposition to selling and promoting junk food in schools has turned into a powerful nationwide movement. Los Angeles was the first city school district to pass a soda ban, which it enacted in 2002. New York City, Philadelphia, Chicago, and others have since followed. As of

During a school taste test, a Pennsylvania student smells a biscuit, one of several items that a food company hopes to sell to her school.

2005, at least eighteen states had passed laws to improve the nutritional value of foods and beverages offered in schools. In many more states, similar legislation is pending. These measures vary widely from replacing soda with healthier drinks to eliminating all foods that are deep-fried in fat. Food companies have lobbied hard to defeat these measures, and most were passed only after major concessions were made to industry groups. Arizona and Louisiana, for instance, restrict the sale of sugary and fatty foods in the lower grades but give high school students more choices. Despite such compromises, supporters say the measures help to reverse years of poor eating habits and nutrition among American schoolchildren.

Truth in Food Labeling

To improve eating habits among Americans of all ages, health advocates also demand greater truth in food labeling. Consumers who walk down the aisles of a grocery store encounter hundreds of packaged products whose labels proclaim they are fortified with essential vitamins, contain heart-healthy whole grains, or help reduce the risk of cancer and other diseases. Shoppers roll their carts past dozens of products marketed as low fat, reduced fat, lite, sinless, or guilt free. If they stop to read the ingredients lists on the packages, they often see confusing words such as dextrose, sucrose, glucose, and high fructose corn syrup, all of which are really just alternate forms of processed sugar. In 1990, Louis Sullivan, then secretary of the U.S. Department of Health and Human Services, complained, "Consumers need to be linguists, scientists and mind readers to understand the many labels they see."[21]

WHO IS TO BLAME?

"Any genuine effort to reduce childhood obesity must attack the problem at its roots. And that means holding the food industry responsible for its role in creating the problem."

Susan Linn and Diane E. Levin, "Stop Marketing 'Yummy Food' to Children," *Christian Science Monitor,* June 20, 2002. www.csmonitor.com/2002/0620/p09s01-coop.html.

In theory the health claims that food companies make on their packages are supposed to be backed by firm scientific evidence. Yet the federal agencies charged with oversight of food labels typically review only the most outrageous and misleading of these claims. This leaves food companies with tremendous freedom in how they market their products. Since consumers are eager to buy foods that protect against disease and promote longer life, companies invest heavily in research and development of products designed just so they can be marketed using health claims. For example, they fortify hundreds of foods, including sugary cereals, fruit juices, and doughnuts, with nutrients such as vitamin C, calcium, and fiber and tout the benefits of these nutrients on their labels. In one instance, when studies suggested that a diet high in whole grains lowered the risk of heart disease, many cereal and snack companies rushed to add whole grains to their existing products. General Mills, for example, reformulated cereals such as Cocoa Puffs and Lucky Charms to contain whole grains. The company did nothing to alter the sugar or calorie content of these products, but the added whole grains meant the boxes could carry a whole-grain banner and a seal of approval from the American Heart Association. Health advocates complained that this gave consumers the false impression that the products were healthful, encouraging them to eat more.

Ironically the lack of clear labeling standards has also allowed food companies to cash in on public fears about obesity and weight gain. The 80 million Americans who are estimated to be dieting at any given time are often willing to pay extra for products that they believe will help them slim down. Many companies have their own reduced-fat product lines, such as Nabisco's fat-free SnackWell's cookies, that are huge moneymakers. Yet nutritionists caution that low-fat and reduced-fat labels are deceiving. People tend to believe that the reduced-fat label gives them a license to eat more, but many of these products contain more added sugar and calories than the regular

Jumping on the nutrition bandwagon, General Mills added healthy whole grains to cereals like Lucky Charms, but the company did not reduce the amount of sugar in these cereals.

A shopper checking out a nutrition label should be aware that low-fat and reduced-fat products may contain more sugar and calories than the standard product versions.

versions. They are just as likely to cause weight gain as any other high-calorie packaged food.

Health and consumer groups want to put an end to this misleading and deceptive food labeling. They call for a simplified format for food labels in which ingredients and nutritional content are listed in language that is easy for consumers to read and understand. They also recommend that companies be forced to use a universal definition of serving sizes so that a single serving means the same thing from one food manufacturer to the next. If the USDA determines, for example, that a single serving of soda is 8 ounces (.24L), then a 20-ounce (.59L) bottle would list 2.5 USDA servings. Advocates propose extending such labeling rules to restaurants, fast-food chains, and vending machines as well. This would force companies such as McDonald's and Burger King to prominently display important information about fat, sugar, and sodium content along with calorie counts on menu boards, where customers could access them without having to search the Internet or request a special brochure stored behind the counter.

Snack and Soda Taxes

In addition to promoting new labeling standards, food-industry critics are looking to borrow a tactic from the antismoking campaign by imposing a tax on soda and junk foods. Most states currently add large taxes to packages of cigarettes, and evidence suggests that these have had a major impact in driving down the rate of smoking. Similar food taxes would force consumers to pay extra for products that promote weight gain and obesity. At least eighteen states have already experimented with taxes on soda, candy, chewing gum, and other snack foods. For the most part these taxes are small and very limited in scope, targeting only a few specific junk-food items. Arkansas, for instance, adds a two-cent tax on each 12-ounce (.35L) bottle of soda.

The idea of larger taxes on snack foods and soda, however, remains extremely unpopular with the majority of Americans. Many people are strongly opposed to new taxes of any kind. Consumer taxes on food products evoke images of a nanny or food police interfering in people's lives and telling them what they can and cannot eat. This is widely viewed as an infringement on personal liberties and freedom of choice.

Food-industry groups have made the fight against snack and soda taxes a national priority. They have mounted aggressive ad campaigns in which they denounce junk-food taxes as government interference in people's private lives. A spokesman for the industry group Center for Consumer Freedom wrote in 2002, "When we begin controlling what people can put into their mouths, there is no end to what might be next."[22]

Several states, including California and Maryland, have tried to impose large snack-food taxes despite the opposition, but these have met with angry resistance from consumers. Such taxes tend to hit poor Americans the hardest, because people with lower incomes rely heavily on packaged and fast foods, especially when they have limited places to buy healthier items. There are also difficult questions about which foods to tax and which to leave untaxed. In the case of the California law, grocery stores received a long list of nearly five thousand taxable and nontaxable food items. In many cases, the distinctions between the categories seemed arbitrary. Popped popcorn was taxed; unpopped popcorn was not. Milky Way bars were taxed, but Milky Way ice-cream bars were left untaxed. The experience proved extremely frustrating to California consumers and business owners alike. They voted overwhelmingly to overturn the snack tax in 1992, just a year after it was passed.

THE GOVERNMENT NANNY LURKS

"Do we want the equivalent of a government nanny lurking in each grocery aisle clicking her tongue at what's in our shopping cart?"

Quoted in Cato Institute, "Warning Labels on Soda Cans? Cato Analysts Warn Against Latest Health Hysteria," July 12, 2005. www.cato.org/new/07-05/07-12-05r-2.html.

The failed experiment in California and other states has forced tax proponents to consider ways to make junk-food taxes more acceptable. Health advocates Brownell and Battle Horgen believe that Americans are more inclined to support taxation when it is used as an incentive to encourage positive change, rather than as a deterrent to negative behaviors. They propose using tax money to help subsidize and reduce prices for healthy foods such as fruits and vegetables. This would make healthier eating more affordable for all Americans and relieve the tax burden on the poor. To eliminate the problem of arbitrary taxation, they suggest that lawmakers tax entire categories of food, such as snacks, soft drinks, and fast foods, rather than singling out specific products. They say that junk-food taxes—if done right—can become an effective strategy in the fight to curb obesity.

Taking the Case Against Big Food and Big Soda to Court

Junk-food taxes and food-labeling reforms are measures that must be debated in state legislatures and the halls of Congress.

Taking Big Soda to Court

As part of a national campaign backed by health and nutrition activists, lawyers plan to bring a class-action lawsuit (one filed by a group of people who all have the same grievance) in Massachusetts against major soda makers. The lawyers, who earlier represented smokers in the battle against Big Tobacco, argue that soda companies have engaged in unfair and deceptive practices by selling soft drinks to schoolchildren knowing that these were harmful to kids' health. They point to research that links soda drinking to increased incidence of obesity and type 2 diabetes. One such study, by Dr. David Ludwig of Harvard University, followed 548 children who were already soda drinkers over two years and found that for every serving of sugar-sweetened drinks the children added to their daily diet, their chances of becoming obese increased by 60 percent. The soda industry denies responsibility for the problem. "We've been selling soda for 125 years and gee, all of a sudden we're the reasons for childhood obesity," argues Ralph Cowley, chairman of the industry group, the American Beverage Association.

Quoted in Michael Blanding, "Hard on Soft Drinks," *Boston Globe Magazine,* Oct. 30, 2005, p. 26.

Some health advocates are also prepared to take the case against Big Food to court. In 2002, two severely overweight girls in New York City made national headlines when they brought a lawsuit against McDonald's that blamed the fast-food chain for their excess weight and elevated risk of disease. One of the girls, Ashley Perlman, was fourteen years old at the time of the suit and weighed 170 pounds. She had been consuming Happy Meals and Big Mac hamburgers three to four times a week since the age of five. Jazlyn Bradley was nineteen years old and weighed 270 pounds. She often started the day with a McDonald's breakfast and returned to the restaurant during school lunch breaks and after school for burgers, chicken nuggets, fries, and soda. The girls' attorney argued that McDonald's food was responsible for his clients' obesity and deteriorating health and claimed that they were entitled to damages (financial compensation).

The American public was unsympathetic. The lawsuit was denounced and ridiculed in the popular media. Late-night comedians joked about the girls' poor judgment and lack of self-control. Editorial cartoons pictured them eating at McDonald's with a gun to their heads to make the point that no one was forcing them to frequent the fast-food chain against their will. In 2003, the judge dismissed the suit. He ruled that it was not the place of the law to protect people from their own excesses. "Nobody is forced to eat at McDonald's," he wrote. At the same time he left the door open for future lawsuits against the food industry by suggesting that the case might proceed under different legal reasoning. In his ruling he referred to Chicken McNuggets as "a McFrankenstein creation of various elements not utilized by the home cook,"[23] and explained that if the health dangers of such foods were not widely known, then under consumer protection laws, McDonald's would have an obligation to warn its customers.

Food-industry groups were outraged by the judge's ruling and immediately launched a nationwide counterattack. Groups such as the Center for Consumer Freedom began an intense lobbying effort to prevent lawsuits against the food industry from going forward. By 2005, twenty states, including Arizona, Colorado, Florida, Georgia, and Michigan, had enacted so-called "cheeseburger laws" that bar people from seeking damages in court from food companies for weight gain and associated medical conditions. In 2006, the U.S. House of Representatives passed a similar measure to prohibit such lawsuits nationwide. The senate would also need to approve the measure for it to become law. Supporters of these laws say they shield businesses from having to spend huge amounts of money to defend themselves against frivolous lawsuits. But opponents contend that there is no legitimate reason to single out the food industry for special protection under the law. "If you market products to children that cause disease, and you do it in a way that conceals the risks from parents," says CSPI executive director and health advocate Michael F. Jacobson, "you may end up explaining your actions to a judge or jury. That's hardly a radical notion."[24]

Food and Soda Companies Respond

The hundreds of food companies that sell and market products in the United States often respond collectively to the threat of lawsuits and policy actions through a small number of powerful groups like the Grocery Manufacturers Association and the Center for Consumer Freedom. These industry groups vigorously deny responsibility for the obesity epidemic and appeal to patriotic values such as personal freedom and consumer choice. When they are threatened with restrictions on advertising their products, they argue that these are an infringement on their constitutional right to free speech. They place the blame for childhood obesity on overly permissive parents who do not monitor their children's diets closely enough, and they suggest that sedentary lifestyles are just as much at the root of the problem as overeating. And they lash out at critics, whom they accuse of being self-appointed nannies and food cops.

In some states, fast food giants like Burger King and other food companies benefit from new so-called "cheeseburger laws."

Yet even as these industry groups insist on their rights to freely promote their products, individual companies have begun to make voluntary changes. These companies are extremely sensitive to the charge that their marketing is to blame for childhood obesity and are eager to be seen as part of the solution. In 2005, food-industry giant Kraft, for example, announced that it would voluntarily ban advertising of some of its high-sugar products, such as Kool-Aid drinks and Oreo cookies, to children under eleven years old. After being heavily criticized in the media, McDonald's stopped supersizing and added healthy food options to its menus, including salads and apple juice or low-fat milk to accompany Happy Meals. Some fast-food chains are sponsoring PE programs in schools and backing public health campaigns that focus on children's fitness. In 2005, McDonald's premiered a series of ads that stress the importance of an active lifestyle. In the ads, a fit and athletic Ronald McDonald is seen juggling fruits and vegetables, riding a skateboard, and rallying a group of neighborhood kids to kick a soccer ball.

Health and nutrition groups view these voluntary changes on the part of food companies with skepticism. They say such efforts should be applauded, but they do not give companies a free pass to continue to engage in harmful practices such as marketing to children or promoting extra-large portions. "The food industry now stands at a critical juncture and may wish to benefit from lessons learned by tobacco,"[25] say Brownell and Battle Horgen. Food companies, in their view, can respond to criticism by attacking health advocates and denying responsibility for the obesity epidemic, or acting in creative and meaningful ways to change.

CHANGING ATTITUDES AND WAISTLINES

Many Americans have become resigned to living in an unhealthy food and exercise environment. They feel powerless to battle the food industry or to change eating habits and lifestyles that have become ingrained. Instead the nation's approach to obesity has always been to focus on treatment. Overweight Americans, and those who perceive themselves as overweight, spend huge amounts of money, time, and energy in an effort to shed extra pounds. They try every diet fad that comes along, from popular high-protein, low-carb regimens to liquid and even popcorn diets. They support a multibillion dollar commercial weight-loss industry that includes companies like Weight Watchers and Jenny Craig and purchase weight-loss drugs and herbal remedies that sometimes endanger their long-term health. A growing number of overweight and obese Americans, many of whom have struggled to lose weight for years, undergo a surgical procedure called gastric bypass or bariatric surgery in which a portion of their fat is cut away and their stomach size reduced. For some people, these weight-loss methods bring dramatic, life-altering results, but a much greater number lose weight temporarily, only to gain it back again later.

Health advocates say that the problem does not simply lie with the individuals who fail to lose weight, but with a culture that promotes unhealthy eating and a lack of physical activity. They argue that it is time to shift the nation's focus from treatment to prevention. This means working to change attitudes, diets, and lifestyles that have become deeply rooted in the American way of life. "It's not going to happen overnight," predicts Arkansas governor Mike Huckabee, who lost 105 pounds after being diagnosed with type 2 diabetes and is working to curb obesity in his own state. "We have to believe that just as we changed attitudes toward smoking and littering and alcohol over time, we can do so [with obesity.]"[26]

The Search for a Cure

America's obesity epidemic has so far resisted easy solutions, but that has not stopped the nation's major pharmaceutical companies from pouring billons of dollars into the search for a cure, or the American public from holding out hope that a quick fix or magic pill lies just around the corner. With more than 1.1 billion people worldwide reported to be either overweight or obese, drug companies are keenly aware that there are enormous profits to be made if they can produce an effective weight-loss drug or medical treatment. The lure of enormous profits helps to explain why there are an estimated two hundred obesity drugs and treatments now in the research or testing stages

An obese patient undergoes gastric bypass surgery, a procedure in which a portion of body fat is surgically removed and the size of the stomach is reduced.

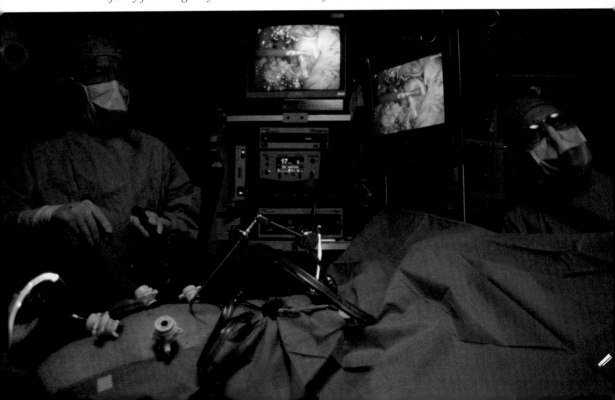

Fen-Phen and Redux: A Cautionary Tale

The popular drugs fen-phen and Redux offer a cautionary tale of what can happen when people look for a miracle cure to solve their weight problems. Fen-phen was a drug cocktail, a combination of two diet drugs that were already on the market, when it was discovered that together they were more effective at diminishing people's appetite and giving them a feeling of fullness. Redux was the trade name for another drug that acted to suppress the appetite. During the 1990s, these weight-loss drugs became overnight sensations. They were rushed to market despite warnings of dangerous side effects. Americans who had struggled to lose weight for years persuaded their doctors to write prescriptions for the drugs, while many more people obtained them without ever seeing a doctor. Weight-loss clinics offered fen-phen to their regular customers. Internet pharmacies sold the drugs to anyone with a credit card number.

Yet fen-phen and Redux eventually became one of the costliest public health disasters in American history. By the time they were pulled from the market, they had caused life-threatening heart and lung problems in thousands of otherwise healthy patients. Dozens of other people had died. The drugs' manufacturers were forced to pay millions of dollars in legal settlements.

in labs and clinics across the country. These include drugs to regulate a hormone that controls appetite in the body, injections that produce a feeling of fullness, and implantable devices that zap electric signals to the stomach or nerve centers when a person is full. Thousands of Americans, desperate to lose weight and relieve the health symptoms and social stigma of being obese, sign up for clinical trials of these new, experimental treatments and drugs every year.

Yet many health advocates worry that this intensive effort to find a cure has taken away valuable resources and attention from addressing the environmental factors that promote weight gain and obesity. They say the best diet advice has not changed in decades. People who want to lose weight and keep it off must do so slowly, by eating healthier foods and smaller portions and exercising regularly. The difficulty for most people is heeding this advice in an environment that places obstacles to healthy eating and exercise at every turn.

Educating Consumers to Make Better Food Choices

One of the first steps in combating the nation's unhealthy food environment and curbing obesity is to educate consumers to make better food choices. Many public health campaigns are already under way to help consumers read food labels, understand portion sizes and calorie counts, and become familiar with the lifestyle and genetic factors that might put them at higher risk for diabetes, high cholesterol, or heart disease. In 2005, the USDA released new, more comprehensive dietary guidelines and MyPyramid, a revised version of the agency's decade-old food pyramid. The new guidelines are aimed at helping people get the

Educating the public about making healthy food choices, including eating more fruits and vegetables, is a primary step in curbing obesity.

Teen girls bounce on a trampoline at a private weight loss camp. Public weight control and nutrition programs do not get much funding.

most nutrients from their calories and discouraging them from eating too many foods high in calories, fat, and processed sugar.

Private and nonprofit groups have also launched education campaigns that stress the importance of healthy eating and nutrition. Former U.S. surgeon general C. Everett Koop is on a mission to teach overweight Americans how to calculate their own weight-related health risks. His Shape Up America! campaign encourages U.S. residents to learn their own BMIs and become familiar with the warning signs associated with unhealthy weight so they can take steps to improve their health.

Yet the funding for public education campaigns like MyPyramid and Shape Up America! are no match for the resources of fast-food chains and snack and soda companies. At its height, the 5 A Day fruit and vegetable campaign, sponsored by the National Cancer Institute, had an annual budget of $2 million for promotion, compared to a $3 billion U.S. advertising budget for Coca-Cola and Pepsi combined. With limited money and resources, efforts like Shape Up America! are unlikely to reach many of the U.S. residents at highest risk for obesity, including poor and minority Americans, recent immigrants, teenagers, and children.

The programs that do succeed in reaching these groups tend to be hands-on and community based. They do not simply admonish people to eat right and exercise, but provide practical support and training to help them make healthier lifestyle choices. *Diabesity* author Kaufman describes one community-based program, called KidsNFitness, that she helped establish in a children's hospital that serves many low-income Latino and African American residents in inner-city Los Angeles. The program enrolls whole families who are struggling with weight gain. They receive intensive practical training on how to navigate grocery stores, read food labels, measure serving sizes, and prepare healthy snacks and meals at home. The program also includes exercise sessions to show that being active can be fun. But even hands-on programs like KidsNFitness face an uphill battle. "The families who participate in this program live in a toxic environment that undermines everything we teach them,"[27] says Kaufman. It is unrealistic to ask most individuals to make heroic efforts to change their own lifestyles, as long as the culture they live and work in remains unchanged.

Creating a Social Movement

Efforts to change the nation's food culture are often met with public indifference. Unhealthy eating has become so ingrained that many people believe it is pointless to resist. Parents who insist on serving only healthy foods at home, for example, are powerless to control what their children eat at school or social events, such as birthday parties. When the family dines out at a restaurant or fast-food chain, they seldom object as their children order from among the unhealthy meal choices on the kids' menu. As a result of the public's indifference, politicians have been reluctant to stand up to the food industry or propose bold policy actions to change the existing culture.

In recent years, however, there have been signs that public apathy about weight gain and obesity is beginning to give way to action. At the local level, parents, health experts, elected officials, and students in some of the nation's largest school districts have joined together to ban soda and junk food from school vending machines and cafeterias. Public and media criticism also has compelled some companies to make changes in the way they do business. Stung by criticism about its role in promoting obesity, Nickelodeon announced in 2005 that it would license several of its most popular characters, including SpongeBob SquarePants and Dora the Explorer, to fruit and vegetable distributors. Parents who open a bag of spinach may find a SpongeBob temporary tattoo inside to encourage their children to eat their green vegetables. The television network also agreed to spend $20 million and devote 10 percent of its airtime to health and wellness messaging. This is far less than food companies spend to advertise on Nickelodeon, but still significant. "If there is any possibility for major social action and policy change," explain Brownell and Battle Horgen, "scientists cannot force it and health leaders cannot mandate it. The public must demand it."[28]

PERSONAL RESPONSIBILITY

"Weight gain can best be tackled person by person, family by family. Take the stairs. Break out the push lawnmower. Choose diet soda. In short, take responsibility. It's not just a good way to go. It's the only way."

The Center for Consumer Freedom, "Personal Responsibility: It's Really That Simple," January 10, 2006. www.consumerfreedom.com/news_detail.cfm/headline/2949.

Focus on Fitness

In addition to improving their eating habits, Americans must also get out of their cars, off of their chairs, and tear themselves away from televisions and computer screens to increase their level of physical activity. Study after study shows that even moderate physical activity improves the health of people in every age and weight range. Such activity does not require elaborate exercise equipment or membership in fancy gyms. Just walking at a normal pace up the stairs, around the block, through a park, or on city sidewalks can improve long-term health. Exercise benefits the heart and reduces the risk of disease. It also helps maintain bone health and may relieve the symptoms of anxiety and depression. For those who are overweight or obese, it is associated with fewer doctor's visits and hospitalizations. Despite these clear health benefits, many U.S. residents find that it is as difficult to stay fit as it is to eat nutritious foods and reasonably-sized portions.

Public-health messages urging people to get in shape help motivate some people, but they are more successful when accompanied by programs and policies that make staying fit convenient and easy. These do not have to be expensive. Some of the most effective fitness programs motivate residents of the same communities to walk and move together. A program called America on the Move, for example, provides information and pedometers (which measure the number of footsteps a person takes) to church groups, schools, walking clubs, health clinics, and work sites across the country and encourages participants

to add two thousand steps per day until they achieve the final goal of ten thousand steps a day. To address parents' safety concerns about allowing their children to walk to school, the Kids Walk to School Project, sponsored in part by the CDC, helps young people walk or bike to school in groups accompanied by an adult. Even the simplest measures can make a difference. Climbing stairs burns more calories per minute than almost any other physical activity, so researchers have experimented with signs posted at the base of shopping mall and subway stairwells with messages like, "Your heart needs exercise; here's your chance." They found that once the signs were up, stair use nearly tripled for both thin and heavier people.

Some employers, looking to save on health costs and increase worker productivity, have also gotten in on the fitness act. They have put into place health and wellness programs that include workplace fitness centers and exercise breaks for employees. For example, the Kansas-based headquarters of the Sprint Nextel Corporation, one of the largest telecommunications companies in the world, was designed with employee fitness in mind. Cars are banned from much of its 200-acre (.81 sq. km) facility. This forces employees to park in garages farther from their offices. Many buildings are separated by walks of as much as half a mile (.8 km) and feature slow-moving elevators to encourage people to use the well-lit stairways instead.

Yet efforts like this are still the exception. Many company headquarters are located along highways or on busy streets where there is no place to walk. New office buildings are constructed with inconvenient, poorly lit stairwells. Employees who walk or bike to work often have no place to wash up or change their clothes. Programs like Sprint's are a positive first step, say Brownell and Battle Horgen, but broader change is necessary: "Times, places, and incentives for people to be physically active must be engineered into daily life."[29]

Making Cities and Suburbs Walkable and Exercise Friendly

Such changes will be challenging to make because most American cities and suburbs were not designed for physical activity.

Seaside, Florida, is an award-winning example of the New Urbanism, where communities are walkable and neighborly.

They were built with cars, not pedestrians, in mind. In some suburbs there are no sidewalks and stores are inaccessible by foot. Suburban residents are forced to hop in their cars, lace up their shoes, and walk around gigantic indoor shopping malls to stay in shape. In many low-income communities, residents worry about the safety of their neighborhoods and parks and rarely walk or jog at all. To overcome these obstacles, health advocates say, the nation must be willing to support innovative programs and commit resources and funding to make cities and suburbs more conducive to walking, biking, and other physical activity.

This is easiest to accomplish when builders start from scratch and design new communities. The architects, urban planners, and health experts who belong to a movement called the New Urbanism are working in several regions of the country to create walkable communities in which residential areas are a short distance from shops and commercial centers. They point to studies that show that people who live in densely populated places that have sidewalks and shops within walking distance tend to have lower rates of diabetes, high blood pressure, heart disease, and stroke. The goal of the New Urbanists is to reduce Americans' dependence on their cars and restore a sense of community to people's lives in order to improve their overall health.

For many existing cities and suburbs, however, it is already too late to realize the New Urbanists' vision. The residents of these communities are unlikely to give up their cars or radically change their way of life. In these places, it is much more practical to encourage walking and biking by adding sidewalks, crosswalks, streetlights, and bike paths to existing roads or a protective strip of parked cars or trees to shield walkers from heavily trafficked streets. Local officials can install bike racks at libraries, parks, schools and other public buildings and hire crossing guards—or recruit parents or other volunteers—to make sure children can safely walk or bike home from school. They can also pass zoning laws and provide tax incentives to builders who construct residential and commercial spaces within walking distance of public transportation.

A HEALTHY LIFE

"We have the opportunity to demand of our leaders, of our healthcare system, of our communities, and of ourselves that the world become a place in which it is possible to live not just a long life but a healthy one."

Francine Kaufman, *Diabesity: The Obesity-Diabetes Epidemic that Threatens America —and What We Must Do to Stop It.* New York: Bantam, 2005, p. 19.

The challenges of improving fitness among residents of low-income, inner-city neighborhoods are even greater. There are many community-based efforts in place, including after-school and sports programs sponsored by local YMCAs, church groups, and community centers. In some cities, vans bring sports gear into low-income neighborhoods and public housing projects to encourage kids to get out and play. Others allow children to take public buses to the local pool or other recreational facilities, free of charge. These small-scale programs have an impact on some people, but they are not likely to resolve the problem of deteriorating health and obesity among most low-income Americans until the issue becomes a national priority. "While there are obviously some costs involved," argues Koop, "the result in terms of reduced health care expenditures will far exceed the dollars spent."[30]

Better Nutrition and Fitness in Schools

Schools are an obvious place to start improving the health and fitness of Americans of all income levels. If children are taught to appreciate the benefits of good nutrition and physical fitness early in their school years, they are likely to carry this with them for the rest of their lives. Health advocates say that there are immediate steps federal and state lawmakers can take to put the nation's public schools at the forefront of a campaign to improve public health. They can call for a ban on all junk foods and soda in school cafeterias and vending machines and find other ways to replace food and soft-drink money. They can ensure that children have enough time to eat lunch to cut down on snacking between classes. They can make the areas around schools junk-food–free zones, where fast-food chains are not permitted. To improve physical fitness, they can mandate that children get at least thirty minutes of physical activity during the course of the school day and provide funding for local school districts to repair playgrounds and purchase sporting equipment.

Local school officials can also play an important role in improving children's health by supporting nutrition education programs in which children are taught to read food labels and understand serving sizes and calorie counts. These programs can include media literacy training in which students learn to recognize and resist the marketing tactics that fast-food chains and snack and soda companies use to appeal to kids. They can also encourage open discussion of cultural attitudes about body image, dieting, and hazardous weight-loss fads and the difficulty of fighting the nation's unhealthy food culture.

Some districts are already going beyond these nutrition basics. They are experimenting with innovative programs in which students grow their own fruits and vegetables or eat locally

Eating and Learning at the Promise Academy

Before they enrolled at the Promise Academy, a public charter school in the Harlem neighborhood of New York City, most of the students had never tasted a fresh raspberry or a peach that did not come from a can. Ninety percent of them came from low-income families and received free or reduced-price lunches as part of the government's school lunch program. Almost half were overweight.

The school's founders believe they can boost students' academic performance and quality of life by first improving their health and nutrition. At Promise, students are served meals like whole-wheat pasta covered with sauteed peppers and squash and turkey lasagna with zucchini. A local chef prepares breakfast, lunch, and after-school and Saturday snacks made from fresh, regionally grown produce and unprocessed food. Seconds on main courses are not allowed, but students can fill their trays with multiple helpings from the salad bar. They can also visit the cafeteria between classes to snack on locally grown apples. "Our challenge," says Geoffrey Canada, the teacher and author who developed the Promise Academy, "is to create an environment where young people actually eat healthy and learn to do it for the rest of their lives."

Quoted in Kim Severson, "Eating, Writing and 'Rithmetic:' A Harlem School Takes the Lead in Introducing Children to Healthy Diets," *New York Times*, September 9, 2005, p. C22.

grown, healthy foods. Nationally renowned chef Alice Waters founded one of the first such programs in the early 1990s in Berkeley, California. The Edible Schoolyard began in a rundown vacant lot near the city's King Middle School. Waters organized students and parents from the school to clean up the lot and convinced the city to donate compost to revive the soil. More than a decade later, King students continue to grow, harvest, and prepare meals with their own tomatoes, corn, lettuce, and collard greens. And Waters's project has inspired similar efforts in cities across the nation.

Other schools are experimenting with nontraditional PE classes in which students are taught to have fun and stay fit for life. Rather than ask everyone in a class to play baseball or kickball, gym teachers in these programs offer a variety of activities from which kids can choose. During a single class, for example, some students may be kickboxing or doing yoga, while others do in-line skating. "You have to give them something fun," says childhood obesity expert Reginald Washington, "something they can be successful at."[31]

Changing Attitudes About Obesity and Body Image

Yet even the most successful school and community efforts to curb obesity have a difficult balance to maintain. They must address the environmental forces that promote poor eating habits and sedentary lifestyles without further stigmatizing overweight

As part of their school's fitness program, students examine a replica of five pounds of human body fat.

and obese Americans or deepening the nation's cultural obsession with body image and thinness. Fitness and nutrition programs that focus too heavily on the dangers of weight gain are
likely to make obese people feel singled out or hopeless, especially if these individuals have struggled and failed to lose
weight. Schools in New Hampshire, Texas, Arkansas, and other
states have begun weighing students and testing their fitness.
Some send home fitness report cards that identify a child's
weight and BMI. Yet in a culture that already emphasizes beauty
and thinness, many parents and educators fear that these measures will only make overweight kids feel more self-conscious.
A national advisory group of educators and children's specialists
say it is a mistake to emphasize weight in school fitness and nutrition programs because "this can contribute to fear, shame,
disturbed eating, social discrimination, and size harassment."[32]

The mixed signals that the culture sends about eating and
fitness have already taken a heavy toll on Americans of all ages.
"Even as kids are bombarded from infancy with messages to
chow down foods that experts tell us are practically guaranteed
to make them obese," says *Consuming Kids* author Susan Linn,
"they—girls especially—are being sold the notion that they are
supposed to be impossibly thin."[33] It is no wonder that many
Americans endanger their health with fad diets, weight-loss
pills, and other harmful diet schemes—or that serious eating
disorders, such as binge and purge eating, are on the rise.

Health advocates say it is critical that policies and programs
aimed at curbing obesity focus on better nutrition and fitness and
not on an ideal body size or shape that everyone must strive to
attain. What the nation needs, says Kaufman, is not a new diet,
but "a new normal," a new way of life in which wholesome eating
and daily exercise become a "comfortable, natural routine."[34]

Introduction

1. Radley Balko, "Living Large: We've Been Misled about the Real Threat Posed by the 'Obesity Crisis'," Cato Institute, November 10, 2005. www.cato.org/pub_display.php?pub_id=5185.

2. Francine R. Kaufman, *Diabesity: The Obesity-Diabetes Epidemic that Threatens America—and What We Must Do to Stop It.* New York: Bantam, 2005, p. 16.

Chapter 1: Weight and Health in America

3. Quoted in TIME/ABC News Summit on Obesity, June 2–4, 2004. www.time.com/time/2004/obesity.

4. Eric Schlosser, *Fast Food Nation: The Dark Side of the All-American Meal.* New York: HarperCollins, 2002, p. 240.

5. Quoted in "Weight Issue Plagues Military, Recruiting," *Boston Globe*, July 14, 2005, p. A5.

6. Kelly D. Brownell and Katherine Battle Horgen, *Food Fight: The Inside Story of the Food Industry, America's Obesity Crisis, & What We Can Do About It.* Chicago: McGraw-Hill Contemporary Books, 2004, p. 6.

7. Paul Campos, *The Obesity Myth: Why America's Obsession with Weight Is Hazardous to Your Health.* New York: Gotham, 2004, p. xv.

8. Rick Berman, "Industry Salivates Over New Cash Cow," *Atlanta Journal-Constitution*, February 23, 2005. www.consumerfreedom.com/oped_detail.cfm/oped/316.

Chapter 2: Why Are Americans Overweight?

9. Campos, *The Obesity Myth*, p. 73.

10. Marion Nestle, *Food Politics: How the Food Industry Influences Nutrition and Health.* Berkeley: University of California Press, 2002, p. 16.

11. Quoted in Ellen Ruppel Shell, *The Hungry Gene: The Science of Fat and the Future of Thin.* New York: Atlantic Monthly, 2002, p. 207.

12. Hardee's, "Charbroiled Angus Beef Thickburgers." www.hardees.com.

13. Brownell and Battle Horgen, *Food Fight*, p. 23.

14. Michael Fumento, *The Fat of the Land: The Obesity Epidemic and How Overweight Americans Can Help Themselves.* New York: Viking, 1997, p. 99.

Chapter 3: Eating Habits and Lifestyle Among American Youth

15. Brownell and Battle Horgen, *Food Fight*, p. 50.

16. Schlosser, *Fast Food Nation*, p. 43.

17. Susan Linn, *Consuming Kids: The Hostile Takeover of Childhood.* New York: The New Press, 2004, p. 100.

18. Kaufman, *Diabesity*, p. 220.

19. Quoted in Michael D. Lemonick, "America's Youth Are in Worse Shape Than Ever, But There's a Movement Afoot to Remedy That," *Time*, June 6, 2005, p. 57.

20. Kaufman, *Diabesity*, p. 243.

Chapter 4: The Role of the Food Industry

21. Quoted in Nestle, *Food Politics*, p. 259.

22. Quoted in Brownell and Battle Horgen, *Food Fight*, p. 266.

23. Quoted in Kaufman, *Diabesity*, p. 219.

24. Quoted in Erin Madigan, "'Cheeseburger' Bills Fill State Lawmakers' Plates," *Insurance Journal*, March 7, 2005. www.insurancejournal.com/magazines/west/2005/03/07/features/52953.htm.

25. Brownell and Battle Horgen, *Food Fight*, p. 296.

Chapter 5: Changing Attitudes and Waistlines

26. Quoted in Geoffrey Cowley and Karen Springen, "A 'Culture of Health': Arkansas Gov. Mike Huckabee Has Put His

State on a Fitness Regimen. Can He Do the Same for America?," in "Designing Heart Healthy Communities," *Time*, October 3, 2005, p. 67.

27. Kaufman, *Diabesity*, p. 204.

28. Brownell and Battle Horgen, *Food Fight*, p. 286.

29. Brownell and Battle Horgen, *Food Fight*, p. 96.

30. Quoted in "Low-Income Americans Face Major Obstacles to Weight Control, New Survey Finds," Shape Up America! October 31, 1995. www.shapeup.org/about/arch_pr/0131 95.html.

31. Quoted in Lemonick, "America's Youth Are in Worse Shape Than Ever, But There's a Movement Afoot to Remedy That," p. 57.

32. Quoted in Frances M. Berg, *Underage & Overweight: America's Childhood Obesity Crisis—What Every Family Needs to Know*. New York: Hatherleigh, 2004, p. 8.

33. Linn, *Consuming Kids*, p. 102.

34. Kaufman, *Diabesity*, p. 185.

DISCUSSION QUESTIONS

Chapter 1: Weight and Health in America

1. How do doctors and scientists measure and track weight gain and obesity in individuals and populations?

2. What are the environmental factors that health experts suggest make residents of poor communities more susceptible to overweight and obesity?

3. Why is it difficult to determine how many deaths are caused by excessive weight gain and obesity?

Chapter 2: Why Are Americans Overweight?

1. How have fast-food chains like McDonald's and Burger King changed Americans' eating habits and lifestyles?

2. What reasons does the author cite for Americans' lack of physical activity?

3. Why do many health experts conclude that environmental and not biological or genetic factors are the main causes of the obesity epidemic?

Chapter 3: Eating Habits and Lifestyle Among American Youth

1. What changes have occurred in children's diets in the past several decades that help explain the rising rate of childhood obesity?

2. What tactics do food companies and fast-food chains use to appeal to children and teens and entice them to buy their products?

3. According to the author, what are the lifestyle factors that make the current generation of American children the least active and most sedentary generation in history?

Chapter 4: The Role of the Food Industry

1. How is the nation's public health campaign against cigarette smoking similar or different from efforts to reform the food industry?

2. What policy measures have health advocates proposed to hold the food and soda industries responsible for rising rates of obesity?

3. How does the food industry defend itself against charges that it has contributed to the obesity epidemic?

Chapter 5: Changing Attitudes and Waistlines

1. Why do many health advocates believe a drug or medical treatment for obesity is unlikely to be effective on a large scale?

2. What does it mean to engineer physical activity into daily life?

3. What are the mixed messages that American culture sends about body image, thinness, and overeating?

ORGANIZATIONS TO CONTACT

American Diabetes Association (ADA)
Attn: National Call Center, 1701 North Beauregard St.
Alexandria, VA 22311
(800) DIABETES (800-342-2383)
www.diabetes.org/home.jsp

The ADA provides diabetes research, education, and advocacy on behalf of people living with the disease.

The American Obesity Association
1250 24th St. NW, Suite 300, Washington, DC 20037
(202) 776-7711 • fax: (202) 776-7712
www.obesity.org

The American Obesity Association is an education and advocacy group that fights discrimination against obese Americans and lobbies government and health groups to treat obesity as a disease rather than a matter of personal failure.

The Center for Consumer Freedom (CCF)
P.O. Box 27414, Washington, DC 20038
(202) 463-7112
www.consumerfreedom.com

The CCF is a coalition of restaurants and food companies that works to promote free-market principles and consumer choice. CCF lobbies against measures such as restrictions on food marketing and snack-food taxes and accuses health advocates of being nannies and food cops.

Center for Science in the Public Interest (CSPI)
1875 Connecticut Ave. NW, Suite 300
Washington, D.C. 20009

(202) 332-9110 • fax: (202) 265-4954
www.cspinet.org

A strong voice in the movement to reform the food industry, CSPI conducts scientific research on nutrition issues and lobbies for measures such as food-marketing restrictions and snack taxes. The group also takes an active role in lawsuits against food and soda companies.

Centers for Disease Control and Prevention (CDC)

1600 Clifton Road NE, Atlanta, GA 30333
(404) 639-3534 or (800) 311-3435 • fax: (202) 265-4954
www.cdc.gov

The CDC, a branch of the government's Department of Health and Human Services, is charged with protecting and improving the health and safety of all Americans. CDC sponsors research on obesity and nutrition issues.

The Edible Schoolyard

Martin Luther King Jr. Middle School
1781 Rose St., Berkeley, CA 94703
(510) 558-1335 • fax: (510) 558-1334
www.edibleschoolyard.org

Founded by renowned chef Alice Waters of Berkeley, California, the Edible Schoolyard provides urban public school students with an organic garden and teaches them to grow, harvest, and prepare fresh produce. The project has become a model for school garden and nutrition projects around the country.

Kids Walk to School

Division of Nutrition and Physical Activity, National Center for Chronic Disease Prevention and Health Promotion
Centers for Disease Control and Prevention
4770 Buford Highway NE, MS/K-24, Atlanta, GA 30341-3717
(770) 488-5820 • fax: (770) 488-5473
www.cdc.gov/nccdphp/dnpa/kidswalk

Kids Walk to School is a community-based program sponsored by the CDC that helps communities organize to create safe routes for children to walk and bike to and from school in groups, accompanied by adults.

McDonald's Corporation

2111 McDonald's Dr., Oak Brook, IL 60523
(800) 244-6227
www.mcdonalds.com/usa.html

The world's largest chain of fast-food restaurants with more than thirty thousand locations around the globe. In 2003, McDonald's started its I'm Lovin' It marketing campaign to promote a new healthier image. In 2006, the company announced that it would include nutritional information on its food packaging and emphasize healthier menu items.

The President's Fitness Challenge

501 N. Morton, Suite 104, Bloomington, IN 47404
(800) 258–8146 • fax: (812) 855–8999
www.presidentschallenge.org

Sponsored by the President's Council on Physical Fitness and Sports, a group of fitness advisers to the U.S. president, this program encourages Americans of all ages to become more physically active.

Shape Up America!

Contact by e-mail request forms on Web site
www.shapeup.org

Founded by former U.S. surgeon general C. Everett Koop, Shape Up America! is a nonprofit organization dedicated to raising awareness of obesity as a public health issue. The group works to encourage sensible eating, increase physical activity, and help overweight Americans improve their health.

FOR MORE INFORMATION

Books

Marjolijn Bijlefeld and Sharon K. Zoumbaris, *Food and You: A Guide to Healthy Habits for Teens*. Westport, CT: Greenwood, 2001. This book for teens is a thorough and straightforward guide on nutrition and health issues such as eating a balanced diet, reading food labels, avoiding diet fads, and staying in shape.

Kelly D. Brownell and Katherine Battle Horgen, *Food Fight: The Inside Story of the Food Industry, America's Obesity Crisis, & What We Can Do About It*. Chicago: Contemporary Books, 2004. The authors of this book are obesity and nutrition experts who strongly advocate public responsibility for changing the "toxic" environment that promotes obesity in America.

Scott Ingram, *Want Fries with That? Obesity and the Supersizing of America*. New York: Franklin Watts, 2005. In this book for young adult readers, Ingram explores issues of obesity in the news, such as fast-food lawsuits and junk food in schools. The book also includes helpful information geared for teens on BMI, calorie counts, and fitness.

Andrea C. Nakaya, ed., *Obesity: Opposing Viewpoints*. Detroit: Greenhaven, 2006. Designed for young adult readers, this is a collection of articles and commentaries that explore controversial issues related to obesity, including the genetic and environmental causes of weight gain and pros and cons of weight-loss drugs and treatments.

Eric Schlosser, *Fast Food Nation: The Dark Side of the All-American Meal*. New York: Perennial/HarperCollins, 2002. This book contains a journalist's highly critical look at the far-reaching impact of the fast-food industry on diet, agriculture, work, and other aspects of life.

Ellen Ruppel Shell, *The Hungry Gene: The Science of Fat and the Future of Thin*. New York: Atlantic Monthly, 2002. Journalist Ruppel Shell explores issues of genes and environment in promoting obesity and takes a critical, in-depth look at the controversial science and politics behind weight-loss drugs and treatments.

Video and DVD

Morgan Spurlock, *Super Size Me: A Film of Epic Portions*. Samuel Goldwyn Films, 2004. Filmmaker Spurlock puts himself on a thirty-day McDonald's-only, no-exercise diet. He eats everything on the menu at least once during the thirty days, orders supersize meals whenever he is asked, and records the results with humor, even as his health deteriorates.

Web Sites

Body and Mind Project of the Centers for Disease Control and Prevention (www.bam.gov). The Body and Mind site is sponsored by the CDC and includes a food and nutrition area with activities, such as a dining decisions game and customized fitness workout for teens.

Don't Buy It! Project (www.pbskids.org/dontbuyit). Part of the *Don't Buy It!* project sponsored by the Public Broadcasting Service (PBS), this site is intended to help young people become media-savvy consumers. An area of the site called "Food Advertising Tricks" explores the tactics food companies use to entice children and teens to buy their products.

KidsHealth (wwwkidshealth.org). The kids and teens pages of this site feature physician-reviewed articles, animations, games, a BMI calculator, and resources on health and nutrition issues. KidsHealth is sponsored by the Nemours Foundation's Center for Children's Health Media, which works to provide up-to-date information on children's health issues.

National Center for Health Statistics of the Center for Disease Control and Prevention (www.cdc.gov/growthcharts). The CDC's National Center for Health Statistics offers the latest data from national health and nutrition surveys on weight gain and obesity and tools for calculating BMI.

Smart-Mouth (www.smartmouth.org). This site is sponsored by the Center for Science in the Public Interest (CSPI), which promotes greater food-industry accountability. It includes articles, healthy recipes, activities for kids and teens, and a "Bite Back" feature that encourages young people to take action by writing to elected officials and food companies.

Take Charge Project of the Weight Control and Information Network (www.win.niddk.nih.gov/publications/take_charge. htm). A guide to healthy living for teenagers sponsored by the Weight Control Information Network (WIN). WIN is a service of government health groups, including the National Institutes of Health. This site includes features on diet, portion size, and exercise that encourage teens to take charge of their own health.

The U.S. Department of Agriculture's MyPyramid (www.my pyramid.gov). This site showcases the USDA's updated food pyramid and dietary guidelines. An "Inside the Pyramid" feature allows users to plug in their age and activity levels and choose the foods and daily calorie counts that are right for them.

PICTURE CREDITS

Cover photo: Taxi/Getty Images
Maury Aaseng, 23
Associated Press, 11, 13, 38, 53, 57, 64, 66, 67
© Richard Bickel/CORBIS, 83
Tim Boyle/Getty Images News/Getty Images, 29
© Fabio Cardoso/zefa/CORBIS, 44
© Najlah Feanny/CORBIS, 72
© John Darkow and Cagle Cartoons. All rights reserved., 34
© Raymond Gehman/CORBIS, 21
© Patrick Giardino/CORBIS, 25
Paul Hawthorne/Getty Images Entertainment/Getty Images, 50
© Janine Wiedel Photolibrary/Alamy, 8

© Karen Kasmauski/CORBIS, 15, 75, 78, 87
© Kim Kulish/CORBIS, 60
© Mike Lester and Cagle Cartoons. All rights reserved. 81
© James Leynse/CORBIS, 31
© North Wind Picture Archives/Alamy, 18
© Jeff Parker and Cagle Cartoons. All rights reserved. 48
Photos.com, 28, 77
© Olivier Pojzman/Olivier Pojzman/ZUMA/CORBIS, 33
© Fred Prouser/Reuters/CORBIS, 62 (inset)
© Roger Ressmeyer/CORBIS, 45
© Lee Snider/Photo Images/CORBIS, 62 (main)
© Tom Stewart/CORBIS, 7

ABOUT THE AUTHOR

Meryl Loonin is a writer with a background in documentary film and television production and a master's degree in education. She has produced and developed many films and television documentaries on topics such as human evolution, Latin American literature, life in the former Soviet Union, and the Cold War race to build the hydrogen bomb. Loonin also has a strong interest in helping young people publish their own work. She has collaborated on Web sites, videos, and books of creative work by and for kids. This is Loonin's third title for Lucent. She lives with her husband, Neil, and two children, Hana and Jonah, in Lexington, Massachusetts, where they walk whenever they can and try their best to battle the food culture.